Advance Praise

Borne out of his own pain ov[...] Coker offers hard-won pastoral wisdom for those who must walk through this particular valley. These reflective sermons are far from theoretical abstractions about pain and suffering; rather, they are deeply theological as he contemplates both the divine and human agency that interplay in every such event. Naming the brutal reality of suicide in church offers a way forward, even redemption.

—Molly Marshall
Retired President
Central Seminary

In the face of suffering, silence comes first in the healing. But when we have to speak into pain, good words are the tools ministers use to shape souls. Jason Coker offers us good words—literally, eulogies or benedictions—that put the heart back into the hurting. *Faded Flowers* should be on the desk of every pastor as a ready resource for our work.

—George A. Mason
Senior Pastor, Wilshire Baptist Church,
Dallas, Texas

Jason Coker's *Faded Flowers* calls to mind Stanley Hauerwas's observation that, in times of great sorrow, what we need is not answers to our questions, but a "community capable of absorbing our grief." In the pages of *Faded Flowers*, we get to watch a community of faith absorb, together, the grief of an unbearable sorrow, and, in the process, learn better how to be such a community ourselves.

—Chuck Poole
Senior Pastor, Northminster Baptist Church
Jackson, Mississippi

There are no easy answers to the kinds of pain Jason Coker confronts in *Faded Flowers*. While his honest and heartbreaking account is rooted in the experiences of a particular community, his words are relevant for just about anyone facing unimaginable suffering. This is highly recommended reading for clergy and laypeople alike.

—*Kenneth Townsend*
Scholar-in-Residence
Wake Forest University School of Law

Faded Flowers is a much-needed resource for clergy working with teens and young adults, particularly on the college campus where suicide is the second-most cause of death. Jason Coker's personal account of his experience of a young man's suicide and its impact on the church community is authentic and compelling. Anyone who finds themselves responding to the tragic loss of a young person through suicide will benefit from Coker's insightful sermons and reflections. Furthermore, he offers us a means to face the complexities of the existence of pain through his scholarly work with the Gospel stories of how Jesus embraced pain during his earthly ministry. *Faded Flowers* is a timely and an important addition to any pastor's library.

—*Mary Grace Williams*
Chaplain of the College/Dean of Community Life
Bard College

When deep pain shows up along life's journey, we often seek solutions for dealing with it while perhaps feeling helpless in its presence. And yet, as fellow travelers in this life, one of the most important gifts we have to give each other is our story. It is through sharing, confession, and witness that we can draw strength, comfort, and a way forward when pain and grief have brought us to a standstill. Dr. Rev. Coker's story is such a gift.

—*Joy Yee*
Pastor, Nineteenth Avenue Baptist Church
San Francisco, California

Faded Flowers

*Preaching in
the Aftermath
of Suicide*

K. Jason Coker

Smyth & Helwys Publishing, Inc.
6316 Peake Road
Macon, Georgia 31210-3960
1-800-747-3016
©2020 by K. Jason Coker
All rights reserved.

Library of Congress Cataloging-in-Publication Data

Names: Coker, K. Jason, author.
Title: Faded flowers : preaching in the aftermath of suicide / by K. Jason
  Coker.
Description: Macon, GA : Smyth & Helwys Publishing, 2020. | Includes
  bibliographical references.
Identifiers: LCCN 2020020689 (print) | LCCN 2020020690 (ebook) | ISBN
  9781641732475 | ISBN 9781641732482 (ebook)
Subjects: LCSH: Consolation. | Death--Religious aspects--Christianity. |
  Grief--Religious aspects--Christianity. | Bereavement--Religious
  aspects--Christianity. | Suicide--Religious aspects--Christianity.
Classification: LCC BV4909 .C63 2020 (print) | LCC BV4909 (ebook) | DDC
  261.8/3228--dc23
LC record available at https://lccn.loc.gov/2020020689
LC ebook record available at https://lccn.loc.gov/2020020690

In loving memory of
Chester "Chet" Wayne Burchett II

July 17, 1989–March 1, 2009

The light of your life still shines bright
in the lives of those who knew you.

Peace, little brother.

Also by K. Jason Coker

The Corporation of God:
A Biblical Critique of Global Capitalism (2021)

Bible and Theory:
Essays in Honor of Stephen D. Moore (co-editor)

James in Postcolonial Perspective:
The Letter as Nativist Discourse

Acknowledgments

This book is a collection of shared grief, love, and goodwill. First and foremost, I want to acknowledge Chet, Marcy, and Garrett Burchett, who lost their son and brother. They have inspired so many people by how they have continued to live out their faith in life-giving ways, both in the immediate aftermath of Chet's death and now. Garrett was in middle school when he lost his only sibling, and it has been my joy to watch him grow and mature. I love this family and am grateful to have been their pastor and friend through such difficult times. I continue to cherish their friendship today.

Christine Browder was a young college student when she came to be my intern at Wilton Baptist Church. The Burchetts opened their home as her host family during her internship. We all loved Christine and saw the call of God in her life that summer, and Chet and Garrett became like little brothers to her. When she learned of Chet's death, Christine immediately flew from Texas to Connecticut, and she became a true colleague in ministry as she helped organize everything around the wake, funeral service, and travel schedules of hundreds of people who came to show the Burchetts love. She stayed a week, working with me to make sure everything happened exactly as it should. I will always be in her debt for that week of her life.

Phyllis Boozer, the chair of our deacons when this happened, was a rock—and continues to be. She helped convene our deacons and organized them into a working machine. Whether she was organizing, making, or delivering meals; transporting people from airports to hotels and back;

washing dishes; guarding doors; or keeping the church on track, Phyllis was masterful and calm. She is a North Star.

The deacons at Wilton Baptist Church completely gave themselves to the tasks surrounding the care for the Burchetts. Extended family and friends from all over the world were overwhelmed with the work that our deacons did and the love that they showed in doing it. I've never been more proud and humbled by a small group of church leaders. In the midst of our loss, the deacons were a true source of ministry for me and for everyone else in our church and beyond our church.

Despite their own grief, members of our church participated in the funeral service for Chet. Our talented minister of music, Todd Beaney, arranged the processional and song of deliverance ("Oh When the Saints") specifically for the service. Pamela Coker and Glynn Funderburk's duet of "Down to the River to Pray" was as beautiful as it was moving. As they sang, so many of us remembered Chet's baptism in that very sanctuary only a couple of years before. Chet's Sunday school teacher, Jim Stockfish, read Romans 8:35-39 and reminded us all that nothing can separate us from the love of God. Jim watched Chet move through middle school and high school as he taught Chet the bedrocks of our faith—and modeled those bedrocks in his own life. Ron Schneier, a fellow guitar player, who loved Chet's musicality, read the Beatitudes from Matthew 5:3-16. I will always be grateful to these church members who made Chet's funeral service so life-giving and full of love; I drew strength from their love. Remembering this service made it possible for me to keep working on this book years later.

I will always love Wilton Baptist Church. It was my first call as a minister to full-time ministry. The people of this congregation nurtured me to deeper faith and taught me how to be a minister. They listened to me week after week as

I learned how to preach and teach. Their love for me and my family made being their pastor a true joy.

The response to our time of trial from the larger religious community in Wilton reminded me of the love that binds the people of God. Temple B'nai Chaim, Wilton Presbyterian Church, St. Matthew's Episcopal Church, Wilton Congregational Church, and the American Institute for Islamic and Arabic Studies all played an important role in making the services possible—chairs from the Congregational Church, personnel for facilities and nursery from B'nai Chaim, Wilton Presbyterian, and St. Matthew's, and love from the Islamic Center. The friendships and deep family connections within this body of believers was a testimony to all that is good in our religions, and the bonds we formed sustained me and continue to bring meaning to my life. I had a standing lunch date every month with Rabbi Leah Cohen and Rev. Dr. David Graybill for nearly a decade. Our Jewish, Presbyterian, Baptist trio continues to bring joy to my life. They have shown me what it means to be a good minister—whether I've been able to follow their lead or not.

Rev. Mary Grace Williams's love and sense of humor enriches my life still. One day in our local Starbucks she told me that grief is one of the great human common denominators. The truth of that statement has knitted me into the fabric of our shared humanity in ways that I couldn't have imagined. I'll always be grateful for her friendship and support.

Rev. Brigitta Remole and Rev. Ken McGarry at the Congregational Church shared so much of this grief with me. From co-hosting suicide prevention seminars to Ken playing a guitar solo for the funeral service, these two ministers shouldered our whole town many times and were partners in ministry on so many occasions that our churches' theology and ethos were barely distinguishable.

Dr. Golnar Sadeghi and Dr. Kareem Adeeb from the Islamic Center prayed for me and our church in ways that we felt. These interfaith and ecumenical relationships were a powerful source of strength in our common humanity. I don't know how I would have made it through this moment without their support.

An important group to acknowledge here is Chet's friends, among them Alex Balionis, John Harakas, Chris Lind, Conor McEneaney, Vincenza Schiano, Dave Sonkin, and Cody Walker, who served as pallbearers. They, along with Chet's girlfriend, Ivy Ross, represent so many of Chet's friends. I loved these kids. They were tough and funny and fun. They loved Chet and he loved them. It was always fun for me to hang out with them after school at Starbucks as they apologized for smoking cigarettes or for "inappropriate" tattoos.

There were kids who grew up with Chet in the walls of our church, and they cheered and supported one another: Michaela Boller, Chloe Cappo, Gabriella Cappo, Haley Cherico, Jon Cherico, Katie Cherico, Ashley Cicalo, Erin Clancy, Lizzy Emond, Jordan England, Morgan England, Regina Foster, Susanna Guffey, Jenny Harris, Matt Harris, Catherine Korostensky, Ali Jones, Sammy von Kühn, Alex Walsh, Clare Zilich, Emily Zilich, and Leah Zilich. They were as much a part of Chet's life as they continue to be in mine.

Friendship makes it possible to move through grief, and when life is good, friendship makes things flourish. I cannot fail to mention some friends who were not a part of our church but have been a part of my life for nearly two decades: Scott Elliott, Jon Schweibert, and Matt Waggoner. These three are New Testament scholars and a philosopher—I've never judged them too harshly for their career choices. I don't see them often enough, but I always know they are there when I need them.

The good people at Smyth & Helwys have been remarkably patient and helpful in bringing this book to fruition. I am grateful for Keith Gammons for accepting this proposal and appreciate his prodding. Leslie Andres saved me from several embarrassments with her editorial eye. She never told me to leave her alone after so many emails. Beyond the publisher and editors, there were others who read this manuscript and gave critical and helpful feedback. Their encouragement in the use of the right word in the right place or the warning against so many adjectives made this book much more readable and meaningful. I am so grateful. I hope, now, this product of many years helps where it is may be needed most: by those struggling with self harm and those who suffer in the aftermath of suicide—I want to acknowledge you, too.

Contents

Preface

This book is a result of a tragic death, a suicide, in 2009. I am finishing it more than a decade later, in the middle of the Covid-19 pandemic, which has voraciously swept across the world, infected almost 6 million, and killed 448,000 people worldwide to date.[1] That number represents both individuals and their grieving families. It's an enormous number of families who have lost loved ones. In the midst of the fear and social isolation that have resulted from this pandemic, the normal issues that devastate life have been accentuated. Those who live in poverty and struggle to find the resources on which to live, struggle more. Those who live in conditions of domestic violence and struggle to survive, struggle more. The same is true for those who suffer with suicidal thoughts.

I can only imagine the pain of families who lose a loved one—no matter the cause—and cannot attend to their dying and dead. Funerals have been the cause of Covid-19 outbreaks in several areas across the country, so families and friends cannot come together to mourn and comfort one another.

This pain is certainly most acute for those who survive and live in the aftermath of suicide.

In this moment, it's hard not to question God's presence in the midst of pain and suffering, but my experience walking through the aftermath of suicide has been instructive. As you will read, my community of faith responded to tragedy in ways that helped me continue to believe in God and God's people. In fact, it gave me a renewed hope in humanity and in God. I hold on to that hope now as we walk through this pandemic, even though we don't know how many more will die or how many more families will suffer in isolation while their loved ones pass from this life to the next. Even with the multilayered and divisive political response to Covid-19, I believe good people will continue to do good in the face of opposition.

While these good people face the challenge of the pandemic, other good people are so sad and scared they may want to give up. For you, who find yourself in this dark place, I want you to know there is help and hope for you—even if you do not believe it or want to believe it. You can find this help and hope very nearby. With a few keystrokes, you can arrive online at the National Suicide Prevention Lifeline at suicidepreventionlifeline.org to find helpful resources and to chat online with a counselor, or you can call to speak with someone directly at 1-800-273-8255. Another great resource is Crisis Text Line. If you are in any type of crisis, text HOME to 741741, and (after two automated responses) a trained volunteer counselor will respond. There are many other good resources by good people who have devoted their lives to help you *right now*. If you are hurting and are contemplating hurting yourself, gently put this down and call the National Suicide Prevention Hotline.

Note

1. This data comes from the Kaiser Family Foundation, "COVID-19 Coronavirus Tracker—Updated as of June 18, 2020," www.kff.org/global-health-policy/fact-sheet/coronavirus-tracker/.

Introduction

In January 2009, I sat down at my desk to think about the upcoming season of Lent. I was the pastor at Wilton Baptist Church in Wilton, Connecticut. I had been there for just over two years but was the associate pastor for five years before that, so I knew the people in the church well and loved them (and vice versa). Though not all Baptist churches do, we observe the liturgical calendar followed by other mainline churches, and Lent is a meaningful season for us. As I contemplated a theme for Lent, I felt God nudging me toward the problem of pain. It seemed to me that pain would be an appropriate (though difficult) theme for a season like Lent. Our church was not dealing with any heavy or burdensome issues, and I thought it would be a good time to work through the issues around pain when few of us were actually dealing with the subject. So off to the theological races I went. I combed through the lectionary, chose the passages I thought were appropriate, prayed for guidance for the sermon topics, and arrived at what follows. Everything seemed to be working out. The chair of our Spiritual Growth and Discipleship Committee took out an ad in the local newspaper so the whole town could hear about this amazing new Lenten sermon series. We may have even had a banner made to put in front of our church. We were poised for a "good" Lent—a reflective Lent when we could "objectively" think through a Christian response to pain.

None of us could have predicted what tragedy loomed in front of us. On March 1, 2009, I preached the first sermon of the series: "Defying Pain." As you will read, the whole thrust of the sermon was to push through pain and hard-headedly do the right thing. I felt pretty good about it, even though no one ran down the aisle afterwards to make a public profession of newfound faith (a hallmark of certain Baptist traditions). Later that afternoon, my wife had taken our two boys on a playdate, so I was home alone when the phone rang. It was the chair of our Spiritual Growth and Discipleship Committee—the one who put the ads in the local newspapers. His voice sounded different; he seemed almost out of breath. Though he had been healthy lately, he had had some heart issues several years before, so I was worried just by the sound of his breathing. Then he spoke, putting words to his breathlessness: "Chet's dead! You have to come. Chet's dead, Jason. Come right now."

To this day, those are the worst words I've ever heard. Chet, their oldest son, nineteen years old, the kid who was in my youth group from seventh grade on, the kid I eventually baptized, had taken his own life at college that afternoon. Chet was one of my favorite kids in a job where you are not supposed to have favorites. He got in trouble more than he should have and ended up having to spend a few weeks in jail a couple of months before he died, but even there he was a bright light, as you will read from the short speech that he gave to our church when he was released. We all loved Chet because he was a kid who always stuck up for the underdog.

He tried to be tough and wear tough clothes and have tough friends, but down deep, Chet had one of the softest hearts anyone could have. He cared for others deeply—his closest friends and family knew this. We will never know what was going through Chet's mind, but he will never be far from our minds and certainly not far from our hearts.

Amid the shocking news and the aftermath, I had to deliver this sermon series on a Christian response to pain. Putting this book together has been a healing step for me. The sermons that follow the first one come from a deep place of questioning as I wondered, "How in the world do I do this?" I loved Chet and love him still, so passing these sermons along with this tragic experience (and all the experiences of the process through Lent) is my attempt to help somebody else who has suffered the pain of intense, inexplicable loss. I lost a beloved friend; Chet's family lost a beloved son, brother, grandson, and nephew. In our loss, we had to listen to these sermons for the next five weeks. I offer them here, hoping that they can help in some way for somebody somewhere.

In addition to the sermons, there are other important segments that help tell a broader picture of what we, Wilton Baptist Church, went through as a congregation. The first chapter, "Jail Tat," is from Chet himself. He had to spend a month in jail from December 2008 into January 2009. During that month, his mother and father and I would visit him separately to let him know we loved him and to check on him. One time I drove to visit him and the correctional officer in charge of visitation that day would not let me in— for no reason at all. I called the chaplain, and he told me there was nothing I could do but come back at a later date. I visited Chet every week during his incarceration except for that week. Another time during a visit, he and I sat in a room together—this was a "contact" visit. Neither of us knew if it was okay to touch each other, so we didn't because we didn't want him to get in trouble. I've always regretted not giving him a hug that day. We were separated by a glass window at every other visit. When he was released, Chet told me he wanted to speak to the church and thank them for their prayers and support. "Jail Tat" is the speech he gave during morning worship on January 11, 2009. We were all proud of him for coming through such a difficult experience and emerging a better person. These would be his last words to us. He went back to college the next week, and seven weeks later his father called me that terrible Sunday. It is important to start this small book with Chet's own words. He was a good kid in so many ways, and that comes through in his speech. He also tells the truth about himself—if he was a saint, he was a rebellious one! And that's one of the reasons so many loved him so much.

Before I preached the second sermon in the series on pain, I had to preach Chet's funeral. I've included that order of service and the sermon in this book because it is probably the most important piece in the whole project. It is incredibly difficult to preach a funeral sermon for a young man who died by suicide. The words you say will affect people for the rest of their lives. They will not forget that funeral. People came from all over the world. Former church members living in Europe, Chet's father's business friends from across the United States, and Chet's friends all came—hundreds of them. He was wildly popular, and his friendship circle was large because he crossed all the teenage social boundaries between jocks and stoners and nerds and whatever else. Over 400 people came to the funeral, and I knew that I had to speak to all of them and that every word mattered. I am grateful to George Mason, the senior pastor at Wilshire Baptist Church in Dallas, Texas, who sent me a sermon outline that included all the best points in the sermon. The sermon was only part of the service, and every part was important. Chet was a guitarist, and Ken McGarry, who had been a friend of mine for nearly a decade by then and had hosted joint youth group events throughout Chet's youth group days, played the Dropkick Murphys' rendition of "Amazing Grace." That song was the postlude for the funeral as Chet was taken out of our church for the last time. It was Saturday, March 6, and it was beautifully bright for a New England spring day.

The next morning, I had to preach the second sermon in the series on pain. The whole week before, since that dreaded call on Sunday afternoon, I had worked feverishly toward the funeral. Former intern Christine Browder flew back to Connecticut to help with everything. She was a true godsend! We were consumed with preparations—making sure the people who were coming would be accommodated with hotel rooms and airport shuttles; ensuring that all the food brought to the Burchetts' house was organized so that the family wasn't crushed by good will; making the funeral home arrangements, food arrangements, pastoral care visits, phone calls, emails, funeral service planning, and an incredible host of other things—that I nearly forgot I had to preach the morning after the funeral. I used all the strength I had not to break down during the funeral service, and I completely neglected to ready myself for the next day. I didn't realize it until I walked into the sanctuary and stood before the church for the opening prayer. As soon as I was on the chancel looking out at the congregation, I began to cry. I didn't even try to stop crying; I was just trying not to weep out loud. It took everything I had as a human being to get through that sermon: "Embracing Pain."

As I look back and reread some of these sermons, I'm a little embarrassed. It may be that I've changed some theologically, but I'm also fairly self-critical. While I was a Baptist pastor in the Evangelical tradition, I feel like some of the sermons were lazy and relied too much on that tradition instead of going deeper into the text and thinking harder about the subject matter. Under the circumstances, I was probably just too tired and deep in my own grief to come up with anything better to say. I'm trying to give myself some grace, and I hope that my failures can give other pastors who have to preach week in and week out, no matter the circumstances, some grace for themselves too. I respond to each sermon with thoughts about what I was trying to say in those moments. In some ways, these responses are my continued attempts to make meaning out of pain but also to add a decade's wisdom I've gleaned from lived experiences.

After the last sermon, I have included the poem I wrote for Chet during the weeks after his funeral. I would visit his grave almost every day for the next year. While those visits have become less frequent over the years, I still return to spend time with Chet. The poem captures many of the things I saw during those first several visits at his graveside along with other things people said to me or about Chet. The commentary on the poem provides the context of my grief and shows how all the small things collect in the recesses of our lives as grief and love struggle for resolution.

The last chapter shows how Chet's death inspired life through the generosity of his family and friends. At the request of his family, our church set up a memorial fund in Chet's name. That fund was created to be used at the guidance and wishes of his family. We were astonished at how much money came in and grateful for how the money was used—and how it continues to make a difference in people's lives.

This book is a small window into the suffering and love of a family, a pastor, a church, and a community. But it is also a window into our lives because we all suffer. Pain is an inextricable part of being human. Suicide is a particularly acute pain that is deeply complicated and confusing for those who are left behind. My hope is that this book is helpful in the healing process for those who are suffering through a similar circumstance. For pastors who find themselves in the terrible place of preaching a funeral for a victim of suicide, may this be a resource for you. For people struggling with grief and pain, I hope this can be a good dialogue partner in your search for meaning. For anyone who feels like they are not worthy of love and who cannot find love for themselves, my prayer is that if you find this book, you at least read and remember this single sentence: *You are loved beyond measure, and your life has meaning for so many others.* If you need help, please find someone right now to talk to in person. Even as I write this, tears fall down my face for you and all the situations that have led you to this point in your life. You matter. Hold on.

1

Jail Tat

Chet Burchett (Chester Wayne Burchett II)
Wilton Baptist Church
January 11, 2009

I spent last month, including my little brother's fifteenth birthday, Christmas, and New Year's, in Bridgeport Correctional Center. I got in a fight for childish reasons a year and a half ago and had to pay the price. First, I just want to say thank you all for your thoughts and prayers. They were felt. My mom, dad, and [pastor] Jason were the people closest to me during this time, and they all kept telling me to use my time in BCC to grow in God. To pray and think about things. Yeah, right. I'm going to be too busy trying to stay safe. Boy, was I wrong. It's not anything like TV; it's still a dark, oppressing, depressing place that can be dangerous, but I had more time than I knew what to do with. I slept a lot, read nineteen books, and wrote letters to my girlfriend every day and still had plenty of time to kill. So . . . I started praying and reflecting and attending the weekly Bible study. Through the course of worshiping—in jail, mind you—and praying, I walked further with God than I have in the last two years on the outside. I kept this to myself, as I do most things. Then Jason told me to write about all my experiences and lessons that I was learning in BCC. I started making a list. I learned how to make a sewing needle out of a battery, how to make "pie" out of saltines and ramen noodles, shoe-laces out of sheets and soapy water . . . among other useless things. I also learned, and this is for the youth who have heard it from their parents and adults a hundred times, that the choices you make when you're fifteen, sixteen, and seventeen can affect your life in ways you don't even realize. The fight that sent me to jail stemmed from bad decisions I made starting freshman year, when I was fifteen.

Go back even further in my life to when I was in sixth grade. I would come home from school with drawings on my hands and arms. My mom hated it! It became such a point of contention that my mom instituted a rule that I had to write a letter to someone for every piece of art on my body. I was twelve years old and I already wanted tattoos. Sorry, Mom, for announcing this to the whole church. Bear with me and I think you'll smile. The whole time I was growing up, my parents said no tattoos. No, no, no. Then when I was sixteen, I came home with my first tattoo. Mama cried; Dad yelled. Which was the standard MO at my house at the time (sorry, by the way). They said no more tattoos or no college. I didn't listen. My mom has cried every time I've come home with a new tattoo. Hopefully this story will be a little redemption.

My latest two tattoos are faith- and family-themed tattoos on my back. She even cried over those. So back to BCC and my stay meaning something . . . I was in the bathroom brushing my teeth and I get a tap on my shoulder: "Hey, brother, where did you get those tattoos done?" I told him, and then he asked about my faith tattoo. I told him that I was a Christian and that my faith and family were two of the most important things to me. He said, "My grandma always told me to go to church, but I was too busy hustling on the streets." I told him to go to the service that night and he did. By the end of it he was crying and shaking and praying such a heartfelt prayer that I had goosebumps. He was thanking God he was locked up. The service ended with talk about how everything happens for a reason, and on the way out the guy said, "Thank God for your tattoos." So, Mom, I told you they weren't that bad. It got me thinking that if such a small thing like a tattoo and a month in jail can make such a big difference in two people's lives, imagine what we could do with a congregation like ours full of people who cared and who didn't judge and who weren't too busy to help. If we just love and live and be open about our faith, we can do ground-shaking, earth-shattering things with seemingly small actions. Thank God for my tattoos. And thank God I spent Christmas in jail.

2

Defying Pain

Mark 1:9-15
Wilton Baptist Church
March 1, 2009

Deep suffering makes theologians of us all. The questions people ask about God in Sunday school rarely compare with the questions we ask while we are in the hospital. This goes for those stuck in the waiting room as well as those in the hospital beds. To love someone who is suffering is to learn the visceral definition of *pathetic*: 1) affecting or exciting emotion, especially the tender emotions, as pity or sorrow; 2) so inadequate as to be laughable or contemptible. To spend one night in real pain is to discover depths of reality that are roped off while everything is going fine. *Why me? Why now? Why this?*

This is how Barbara Brown Taylor opens her article "Our Bodies, Our Faith: Practicing Incarnation" in a recent edition of *Christian Century*.[1] She raises the question that believers in

God, especially Christians, have asked for eons. Why do bad things happen to good people? Why do bad things happen to me? Why do bad things happen? It's the problem of *pain*, and this problem has a technical name because it is such an age-old issue: theodicy. How do you reconcile the existence of pain or suffering or evil with the existence of God? How can a God who is all powerful, all knowing, and all good exist at the same time as such human misery throughout human history?

In his introduction to *The Problem of Pain*, C. S. Lewis acknowledges this as a philosophical hang-up he had when he was an atheist: "Either there is no [God] behind the universe, or else a [God] indifferent to good and evil, or else an evil [God]."[2] At the time for Lewis, it was philosophically illogical for an all-good, all-knowing, and all-powerful God to do nothing while the world that the same God created destroyed itself. After Lewis became a Christian, this issue raised its ugly head when his wife died. In *A Grief Observed*, Lewis agonizes over the death of his wife: "Sooner or later I must face the question in plain language. What reason have we, except our own desperate wishes, to believe that God is, by any standard we can conceive, 'good'? Doesn't all the *prima facie* evidence suggest exactly the opposite? What have we to set against it?"[3]

Today and for the next five weeks we will be dealing with the problem of pain through the season of Lent. This season of fasting that the church has set aside for centuries in order for Christians to focus their lives provides us a pertinent moment to deal with an all-important issue. Pertinent because there are people suffering right here in our church family—suffering from illness, broken relationships, lost jobs, barren job markets, empty banking accounts, and empty promises. And we are not alone. Right now in our national conscious-ness, we are feeling the squeeze and we are looking for a way out. Right now people all over the world are searching for meaning in the midst of trying times. During these times, people seek religion and spirituality to fill the void that has been left by the hollow tombs of consumerism and materialism. The paradox of it all! People turn to us, the church, for answers, and quietly we know their questions all too well. Their questions are ours! Why me? Why now? Why this?

Pain, suffering, sorrow, and the like are shape-shifters that take on many faces: poverty, loss, illness, divorce, death, separation, incarceration, betrayal, and so it goes. This is why pain is a lowest common denominator in what it means to be human. If there are universal truths, pain is one of them. It is an inevitable part of the human condition. No religion or ideology spares anyone from pain. It is such a profound human experience that almost all authors since the beginning of written language have been writing about it. The first Western epic, Homer's *Odyssey*, is full of pain and sorrow. When was the last time you read a book or watched a movie that had absolutely no pain in the plot? It goes without saying that the books and movies we like the most, and the books and movies that win the most awards, are those that have tremendous pain but an ultimate triumph over it, right? We love stories where the good guys win in the end! We love them because it is what we want more than ever to happen in our own lives. We want to overcome sickness, we want to triumph over evil, we want to dance all over destruction, and we want to wipe away tears. We want this because all of us know too well what pain and suffering are like.

So how do we respond to pain? That is a remarkably different question from "Why me? Why now? Why this?" We will pay attention to the *why*, but we want to concentrate on the *how*. How do we respond? How do we face pain as Christians? I came to this series of sermons as I sat in my office reading the lectionary texts for Lent. In every text from now until Palm Sunday, Jesus' death is mentioned, or he faces some type of tragedy. In every passage from now until Palm Sunday, Jesus deals with his own mortality. In our passage this morning, he is driven into the wilderness to be tempted by Satan for forty days! Immediately following this verse, it says that his cousin, John the Baptist, had been arrested—and we know that this will end with John's head literally on a platter. This passage says nothing about how Jesus handled the news or about how he handled the temptation by Satan. We are left to guess at how this affected him. But it is hard to imagine that these two remarkable events left no impression on Jesus. They were painful, sorrowful, and difficult experiences in their own right. Matthew tells us more details about Jesus' temptation in the wilderness and how he triumphed, but even there we are not told how difficult it was for Jesus to come to a resolve on these temptations. I suppose they were life changing. I suppose if Satan tempted me while I was all alone in the desert for forty days, it would most likely define my life. However, we are not given this privileged information about the psychology of our Savior. We are only given the next verse: "Now after John was arrested, Jesus came to Galilee, proclaiming the good news of God, and saying 'The time is fulfilled, the kingdom of God has come near; repent, and believe in the good news'" (Mark 1:14). In this Scripture, in this case, how did Jesus respond to pain?

He defied pain. This has already got the plot of a good story; it almost makes you want to read the Bible! Jesus defied pain. He had a total disregard for it! After being alone for forty days in the wilderness except for Satan who was tempting him, Jesus came home to the news that his cousin, who had baptized him only forty-plus days before, was arrested. And what did Jesus do? He came to Galilee proclaiming the good news. Before you think I will offer this example as a way we are supposed to respond to pain, let me say this: Jesus responded to pain in different ways at different times for different reasons. In *this* passage, Jesus defies pain. We will learn over the next five weeks that in some cases Jesus embraces pain, he confronts pain, he relieves pain, and he redeems pain. But today, in *this* passage, Jesus defied pain. So this passage in Mark offers us one example of how we can respond to pain. In some cases and at some times in our lives, we are called to defy pain—to disregard it. I'm not sure how this will look in your particular instance. You have to figure out what that will look like. You have to figure out whether your place in life requires defiance or some other response. But today, brothers and sisters, we will defy pain.

We will stand up in the midst of our suffering—in the midst of our situation—and we will tell pain, we will tell sorrow, we will tell evil, *you are not the boss of me!* You will not dictate my life, you will not dictate my reaction, you will not govern my emotions, you will not hold me down, you will not hold me back—you will not! Today, we will take Jesus' example and we will defy pain. *How?* That's a fair question. How do we do it? How do we defy pain? How do we disregard something that cannot be ignored? I have a terminal illness; how can I defy that? I am in a horrible relationship with my spouse; how can I defy that? I live in abject poverty or have just lost my job; how can I defy that?

Jesus defied temptation and incarceration with good news. He defied pain with the good news of God. In spite of all our circumstances, in spite of the real pain and suffering we face, in spite of our human condition, in spite of pain being a universal truth, there is *still* good news. God is good, *all the time!* God is good, *all the time!* God is good, *all the time!* All the time, *God is good.*[4] How did Jesus defy pain? He knew that someone else was there with him in the desert besides Satan. He knew that God was with him, and God is good. How did Jesus defy pain? He knew that someone else was with his cousin in that jail cell, and I'm not talking about a cellmate. God was with John the Baptist, and God is good. There will be days when our response to pain will be different. But today we will defy it because we know that God is good all the time. All the time, God is good. In the Bible, Jesus says, "I will be with you always, even until the end of time." Just as children run to their parents when they experience pain, so will we run into the arms of our loving God. We will sit in God's presence and know that God is good. This is how we will defy pain. Amen.

Defying Pain (A Response)

I never anticipated these sermons would be a resource for pastors or others who may be dealing with a crisis such as suicide. My only goal at the time was to provide as much meaning as possible to a particular congregation in a particular place during the season of Lent in 2009. The event that happened three hours after I preached this sermon dramatically changed all the sermons that followed this one in this series—and probably every sermon I have preached since then. When a tragedy like suicide happens in your congregation, it shifts everything. It is not something a congregation or an individual "gets over." A death like this changes a congregation, and it changes an individual—and I think that's the way it is supposed to be. The whole world is different because someone you love is gone. Nothing fills that void. While everyone tries to heal from such a loss, we carry the scar of the missing. While we were on a mission trip in the Mississippi Delta, a mother who had lost her son to a car accident told our group that losing her son was like a thousand-pound block of ice that sat on her heart. Over the years the ice slowly melted, but it only melted down to a ten-pound block of ice. She said she carries that block of ice forever. While this is certainly anecdotal, it was true to her, and it has been true for many of us who remember Chet.

I don't know if I could ever write this sermon again. To be honest, I believe in it less than I did when I wrote it. To defy pain sounds strong and powerful, but when the pain that we suffered so soon after this sermon was so acute, defying it seemed impossible. It was impossible, which is why I'm grateful it was the first sermon in the series. As a Baptist, I always feel obligated to the biblical text as a point of reference, so I was certainly trying to be faithful to the text of Mark 1:9-15.

As the first sermon in a series on theodicy, it was important to start with the overarching question that all the rest of the sermons were going to address. The first sermon in a series always has to do this double work: introduce the entire series as well as provide a real sermon with its own point or points. As you can see, half the sermon discussed the overall problem of theodicy and the second half focused on the title of the sermon: defying pain.

Theodicy deserves much more than half a sermon; indeed, it deserves much more than an entire sermon series. The term itself literally means "justifying God." That's exactly what those who believe in God must do in the face of human suffering. We are faced with justifying why God would do nothing in the face of human suffering, or why God would allow bad things to happen. If someone takes their faith in God seriously, she or he will have to spend real time contemplating this predicament. As a pastor or preacher, it is even more important to form some kind of provisional answer to this problem because you will deal with pain all the time. The first tenet of Buddhism is powerfully true: all life is suffering. Pastors deal with human suffering all the time through pastoral care, pastoral counseling, and in sermons.

In the process it is okay to believe and say that God is big enough to withstand our scrutiny in this line of questioning.

There is not a real answer to this question, and be leery of anyone who thinks they have an answer. One of the best reckonings with the question comes in James L. Crenshaw's book *Defending God: Biblical Responses to the Problem of Evil.* While Crenshaw's book exclusively focuses on the Hebrew Bible, his conclusions are important for anyone dealing with this question. In the end, and after important and informed readings of the Hebrew Bible, Crenshaw turns the question back to us:

> Regardless of the theodicy that we choose, one thing is certain. Both God and humankind present problems. Theodicy therefore has a twin—anthropodicy. Any attempt to justify human conduct must confront evidence of evil every bit as horrendous as the evil we would see on the part of God . . . . Still, a purely negative assessment of the human community, like a straight verdict of guilt for the deity, must be judged myopic in light of the redeeming goodness of a few. That quality, like evil itself, defies explanation.[5]

Crenshaw's work is important for the overall question of theodicy and worth the time to read the whole book, but his turn at the end may be most significant for pastors who must consider this question in depth. There is a human responsibility in evil and suffering—both in the cause and healing. Paying close attention to our actions may help us determine which course we are taking. This dark side of our humanity is always there. To ignore it or deny it is to not take theodicy and its twin—anthropodicy—seriously. As one deals with the specific issue of suicide in personal terms, these questions take on much more importance as one attempts to put this pain into the context of faith.

After summarizing the larger project in the extreme, I move on to the point of the sermon for the moment: defying pain. Each of these sermons is based on Jesus' particular response to his own death or harrowing experience in that passage. The lectionary passage for this sermon was Mark 1:9-15, which is the typically rapid Markan accounts of Jesus' baptism, temptation in the wilderness, John the Baptist's arrest, and the beginning of Jesus' Galilean ministry. I take advantage of Mark's immediacy by focusing on the fact that the narrative has Jesus preaching right after what has to be traumatic experiences—his forty-day temptation in the desert by Satan (v. 13) and John's arrest (v. 14a). This is a quick exegetical jump to be sure—almost as quick as Mark's movement through his own narrative. I don't regret the focus of this sermon, but I wish I had spent more time with this given what followed that afternoon. I am glad I said that "Jesus responded to pain in different ways at different times for different reasons" before I said his response in this passage was defiance. It is this supposed act of defiance that fills out the rest of my sermon.

I want to make an important distinction between "defiance" and "denial." I use "disregard" as well, which may be too close to "denial." In moments of crisis, some may choose denial as a response. I don't blame or judge anyone who finds themselves in this situation. Denial, however, is a dangerous place. To deny reality in order to lessen pain and sorrow is a denial of truth that will eventually return with greater force. This defense mechanism attempts to mediate trauma but can distort reality in a way that causes more damage than it mediates. Denying an addiction, for instance, does not mean there is no addiction. It only allows an addiction to remain while it slowly destroys one's body and life. Denial postpones the inevitable and can be more ruinous in the long term. This is not what I was trying to communicate as a model for what to do when experiencing pain or suffering.

Defiance is different. It does not deny reality; it challenges reality. This is not always the best strategy when facing difficult circumstances, but it is definitely *a* strategy. While this sounds like I am trying to defend this sermon from the seriousness of the events that followed it, I admit that it truly falls flat in the face of any death, much less the suicide of a loved one. This part in particular felt so good to preach, but now is nearly embarrassing: "We will stand up in the midst of our suffering—in the midst of our situation—and we will tell pain, we will tell sorrow, we will tell evil, *you are not the boss of me!* You will not dictate my life, you will not dictate my reaction, you will not govern my emotions, you will not hold me down, you will not hold me back, you will *not!*" In our lived reality only hours later, these words lost all potency. Even reading them now makes me shake my head. Major crises *will* dictate your life—not forever, but for a while, to be sure. It is okay to be marked by a traumatic experience, but we always have to move toward healing. It's important to have a level of resilience in the middle of crisis. This may not be "defiance" as such, but resilience gives us a deep understanding that our pain can be healed. This is a place where faith can be profound. I saw this in some brave people after Chet's death.

"Defiance" sounds strong and even radical in the face of pain. But sometimes the pain and suffering are just too big and defiance isn't the correct action. Maybe there are times and places and circumstances where defiance could work. Jesus certainly preached "immediately" after hearing about John's arrest. But was that defiance? Maybe. I certainly didn't feel defiant the very next Sunday when I had to preach the day after preaching the funeral sermon. Defiance wasn't the word or that action at all. I was just trying to not cry audibly as I lead the Sunday morning worship. I had none of what Jesus had when he preached his inaugural sermon. I was just trying to get through it.

Notes

1. Barbara Brown Taylor, "Our Bodies, Our Faith: Practicing Incarnation," *Christian Century*, January 27, 2009, www.christiancentury.org/article/2009-01/our-bodies-our-faith.

2. C. S. Lewis, *The Problem of Pain* (1940; repr., San Francisco: Harper San Francisco, 2001), 3.

3. C. S. Lewis, *A Grief Observed* (1961; repr., San Francisco: Harper San Francisco, 2001), 29.

4. In some traditions, specifically Baptist traditions, this is a call and response, where the preacher says the first part and the congregation responds with the words in italic. As an oral tradition, the call and response in written form may not communicate quite the same emotion it evokes in the preaching event.

5. James L. Crenshaw, *Defending God: Biblical Responses to the Problem of Evil* (New York: Oxford University Press, 2005), 195. For an excellent and shorter analysis of the question of theodicy from a theological perspective, see Daniel Castelo's *Theological Theodicy* (Cascade Companions 14; Eugene, OR: Cascade Books, 2012). Mark S. M. Scott has an important contribution to this conversation by showing the provisional aspect of the dialogue rather than having static answers in his *Pathways in Theodicy: An Introduction to the Problem of Pain* (Minneapolis: Fortress Press, 2015). While not specifically related to the issue of theodicy, Charles E. Poole's book of sermons *A Church for Rachel: Sermons for Those Who Mourn* (Macon, GA: Mercer University Press, 2012) speaks directly to the depth of pain in human existence and probably does more to equip a pastor for pastoral care than any of the aforementioned books.

3

Irresistible

Funeral Service for
Chester "Chet" Wayne Burchett II
Matthew 5:6-13
March 7, 2009
Wilton Baptist Church

Welcome and Invocation

We are gathered here this morning under a dark cloud of sorrow to mourn a son, brother, and friend whom we loved so deeply. Chet's appetite for life, however, was wonderfully huge, so we also gather this morning to celebrate a young man whom one adult friend called irresistible—irresistible, indeed. Some of you have traveled from Europe and all across the United States. On behalf of Chet's family, I say with deep gratitude, thank you for being here. To all of Chet's closest friends, you are most welcomed here now and in the days, months, and years to come. He brought many of you here before today, and that's why I know so many of you. Thank you all for your presence.

The range of emotions felt in this room today stretches deep and wide: from sorrow to shock to anger to grief to guilt to fear to shame to disbelief to worry to wonder. I can only tell you to allow yourself to feel them all, and as you do to offer them up to the only one who is able to do anything good with them—the God who loves you and who loves Chet even now with an everlasting and unfailing love. While our minds and hearts will race with remembrances of Chet and questions of why things came to pass the way they have, I urge you to allow the hymns and songs and prayers and words of Scripture to sink into your soul and grant you the peace that only God can give.

Our thoughts and prayers are especially with Chet's family—Chet, Marcy, and Garrett—and with many other family members and friends who feel today that a part of themselves has died; in a way it has. But wherever there is grief, there is God; and wherever there is God, there is grace; and wherever there is grace, there is gratitude, too. And we shall be looking for that above all today. Please pray with me.

Opening Prayer

Lord of all, as the rhythm of the music beats in our hearts and the words of Scripture sink into our souls, we ask for your comfort in this time of pain. We lift our sorrows to you, asking for your soothing touch. The awful absence we feel with the loss of Chet seems overwhelming, but in our time of great sorrow, God, we know you are with us. And as we sit here this morning in your presence, we offer you, of all things, thanks. Thank you, Lord, for not abandoning us in our time of need. Thank you, Lord, for giving us your love and presence when we need it most. And most of all, God, we give you thanks for all the memories that we have and will continue to cherish of our most beloved friend, brother, and son, Chet. We are able to offer this prayer and this thanksgiving only because we believe in the one who said, "I am the resurrection and the life; those who believe in me, though they are dead, yet shall they live, and whoever lives and believes in me shall never die." We offer our prayers in the name of the one who is high and lifted up, sitting at the right hand of God Almighty, the maker of heaven and earth, Jesus Christ, to whom be all glory now and forevermore. Amen.

Who Was Chet?

In the opening chapter of Jack Kerouac's *On the Road*, the narrator says,

> The only people for me are the mad ones, the ones who are mad to live, mad to talk, mad to be saved, desirous of everything at the same time, the ones who never yawn or say a commonplace thing, but burn, burn, burn like fabulous yellow roman candles exploding like spiders across the stars and in the middle you see the blue center-light pop and everybody goes "Awww!"[1]

That's Chet to me! I met him when he was twelve years old and in seventh grade—a month later he was calling me to get him out of trouble! And so it goes. He was a great guitar player and lyricist and was becoming a great studio engineer. I told his parents one time that I know they didn't approve of many things that he wrote, but he was an amazing poet. He could write, and he got that from his parents.

His friends have called him many things, but they have told me that Chet was genuine, honest, faithful, stubborn, charismatic, silly, and goofy. All of us who knew him well know how much weight these words carry when describing Chet. I've heard stories this week about him ruining a friend's guitar in an attempt to fix it and being very proud that he was only one wire off. I've heard stories of locking keys in a running car at three in the morning, midnight motorcycle rides to KFC, magic tricks to cheer up a friend who was sad, and a four-hour episode of hiccups that took a lot to fix. There is even a kid sitting on Chet's initials right now because they are branded on his rear end! I will not mention his name but his own initials are "JJ." Chet was loved because he loved so freely. Chet understood the inclusiveness of Christ. He was always prone to casting a wide net, and he always brought his friends to church—if they would come. When he had heated debates about religion with friends, I would usually get a phone call or email asking me to back him up.

But there are two stories that act as parentheses around his all-too-short life. Marcy told me that when he started school as a child, Chet was always running out of school supplies. She lost count of how much money she was spending on her son because of his inability to keep track of his stuff. She got so frustrated that she asked his teacher what was happening to all his school supplies. The teacher told Marcy that Chet wasn't losing his school supplies but that he would give them all away to kids who didn't have enough of the supplies they needed. That's Chet!

The other story is more recent. Chet's father, "Big Chet" as he is known around here, told me that when Chet went away to school in Boston for college, he would pass a homeless guy every day as he went to and from school. Eventually, Chet got tired of ignoring him, so he decided to take his guitar and sit with the guy and play music for him. After a while, passersby began to give him money for the music. Chet let the guy keep the money. That's Chet!

Bigger Picture

"They say that you are hate but you are really love. This is our fate coming from above." This was Chet's mantra with his girlfriend, Ivy Ross. It echoes the depth of Chet's character in poetic terms that helps us think about the big picture. What is the big picture? Two years ago, Chet made a public profession of faith in Jesus Christ. In spite of the circumstances of today, Chet got it. I had moved to Texas at the time, and through some remarkable and even divine scheduling, I was able to come to Connecticut and baptize Chet, just right there. I had been with Chet on youth events when he would cry because he didn't feel God and he wanted to. I would always tell him, it's not about feeling; it's about faith. He settled on the faith part in 2007 when he literally became a believer. But it wasn't until this past Christmas holiday that Chet got the "feeling" part. On January 11, Chet stood right where I'm standing now and spoke to our congregation. We didn't know that it would be among the last things we would hear him say. This is how he ended his sermonette:

> I was in the bathroom brushing my teeth and I get a tap on my shoulder: "Hey, brother, where did you get those tattoos done?" I told him, and then he asked about my faith tattoo. I told him that I was a Christian and that my faith and family were two of the most important things to me. He said, "My grandma always told me to go to church, but I was too busy hustling on the streets." I told him to go to the service that night and he did. By the end of it he was crying and shaking and praying such a heartfelt prayer that I had goosebumps. He was thanking God he was locked up. The service ended with talk about how everything happens for a reason, and on the way out the guy said, "Thank God for your tattoos." So, Mom, I told you they weren't that bad. It got me thinking that if such

a small thing like a tattoo and a month in jail can make such a big difference in two people's lives, imagine what we could do with a congregation like ours full of people who cared and who didn't judge and who weren't too busy to help. If we just love and live and be open about our faith, we can do ground-shaking, earth-shattering things with seemingly small actions. Thank God for my tattoos.

Moving On

I don't want to ignore the fact that Chet did not always make the right decisions. In fact, the thing that would frustrate me the most about him was the fact that I thought he tormented his parents too much. I would tell him this all the time. This was the pattern: he would get into trouble, I would talk to him about it at Starbucks and figure out a punishment, we would go to his parents, and usually they would reduce the sentence. I never figured out why he liked me so much when I was so much meaner to him than his parents were. But here we are. And now the question is, where do we go from here? What do we do? I'm not sure, but here are some thoughts.

God does not judge a person's whole life by the last worst decision they make, and neither should we. Jesus makes a profound statement in the New Testament when he says to those who are passing judgment on a woman who has sinned, "Those without sin cast the first stone." We would do well to remember Jesus' words as we remember Chet. So forgive Chet, first of all. Don't excuse what he did. Don't pretend everything he did or failed to do was good if it was not, but let him go, let him rest in peace now. Nothing is left to be gained and so much is lost if you hold bitterness close at heart. Forgive yourself next. Some of you wonder, what if you had done something different—as if it were within your power to change things. Even if it were, it is what it is. There is nothing you can do to change that by blaming yourself or anyone else. Finally, forgive each other. Do not let one tragedy be compounded into others. Do what you know makes for peace and well-being. Consider all relationships and begin to do your part to set them right.

These are baby steps that we can take right now to help us learn how to live with such a tragedy. There's a long road ahead paved with more tears, but those tears will slowly change to tears of happiness for the gift of life that we all had the privilege of sharing with Chet, even if short. When I baptized Chet, I said what many Christian ministers say when they immerse an individual for baptism. As I lowered him into the water, I said, "Chet, you are buried with Christ in baptism." And as I lifted him out, I said, "And you are raised to new life to walk with him." Today we are confident that Chet's new life is with a heavenly host who rejoice for his presence with them. So my prayer is that we may have the capacity to rejoice with those in heaven. Please bow in prayer with me.

Closing Prayer

Lord of heaven and earth, one who does not distinguish between this life and the life after, you know us all from the inside out. You know when we sit and when we stand. You know the words on our lips before we speak. You know the intricate movements of our universe. And you love us all as your own children. As we continue to grapple with our own pain, Lord, send your Holy Spirit to minister to us all. Help us to hold each other close and deepen the friendships and relationships that we have. Help us to talk openly about our difficulties knowing that a sorrow shared is a sorrow lightened. And, most of all, help us to pay more attention to your divine work in our lives, because if there is anyone or anything that can help us through this, Lord, we know it is you alone. And so, with weak and yet thankful hearts, we offer our prayers to you, praying the prayer that you taught your disciples, saying:

Our Father who art in heaven, hallowed be Thy name.
Thy kingdom come, Thy will be done on earth as it is in heaven.
Give us this day our daily bread, and forgive us our trespasses, as we have forgiven those who trespass against us.
And lead us not into temptation, but deliver us from evil.
For Thine is the kingdom and the power and the glory forever. Amen.

Graveside Words

We are grieving, but the bedrock of our faith is a promise from Jesus Christ: "In this world, you will have trouble, but take heart; I have overcome the world." We don't know why we have to be here today, but we will hold our heads up because our faith is larger than our circumstances and our belief is deeper than our sorrow.

Prayer of Dedication

Into your hands, O God of Grace, we commend our loved one, Chet Burchett. We know now that he hears the music of heaven and angels. We know now that he rests eternally in your amazing grace. We know now that he sees you face to face. His sorrow is no more, his pain is long gone, his suffering has ceased. Chet is with you and you are with him. We send him to you now with only love and good will and ask that you mend our broken hearts for our brother who is in your eternal rest. Let us never forget, Lord, the love we have shared with Chet. Let us never forget, Lord, the many days of laughter that we have had together. Let us never forget, Lord, our irresistible son, brother, and friend. In the name of Jesus Christ, who lives and reigns with God Almighty and the Holy Spirit, one God, now and forever. Amen.

Note

1. Jack Kerouac, *On the Road* (London: Penguin Books, 1959), 5–6.

4

Embracing Pain

Mark 8:31-38
March 8, 2009
Wilton Baptist Church

> We spend a good portion of our lives working diligently to acquire those things that make life rich and meaningful—friends, a spouse, children, a home, a job, material comforts, money, and security. What happens to us when we lose any of these persons or things, which are so important to us? Quite naturally we grieve over the loss of anything important. Sometimes, if the loss is great, the very foundations of our life are shaken, and we are thrown into deep despair.[1]

I think in instances of great loss, this deep despair is common for understandable reasons—pain hurts. I had a friend tell me this week that the reason pain hurts is because we are not created to experience pain. When God created Adam and Eve, God created them to be perfect and live forever. God did not create the first human beings to die and grieve. And, he said, that's why we are so ill equipped to face such remarkable circumstances. They never were supposed to happen in the first place. Good theology or bad theology? I don't know, but I like it! For some reason that sounds right—at least to me. That might be why it's so incredibly hard to respond to deep sorrow.

As we continue this sermon series on the problem of pain and our Christian response to it, we shift gears today. Last week's challenge to defy pain seems painfully weak now. But I saw that defiance in so many of you this past week as we faced devastation with stubborn determination. You fought through your tears to be strong for the Burchetts even when you were hurting. You put legs on your prayers every time you prepared a meal, cleaned a table, set up a chair, parked a car, washed the dishes, or washed the clothes and folded them! You defied pain; but that was last week's sermon and we have learned a lot about pain since last Sunday. I hope to God we don't learn as much this week! So the challenge for us today is not to defy pain—though that has its place. Our challenge this morning may be harder, unfortunately. This morning our Christian response to pain will be to embrace it. Embracing pain: a novel idea but one we are not used to.

Embracing pain. In our passage this morning from Mark, Jesus said he would undergo *great suffering, rejection, and death.* Peter tried rejecting this by rebuking Jesus, but Jesus rebuked Peter and said that this path must be embraced not only by the Son of Man but by all who follow him: "If any want to become my followers, let them deny themselves and take up their cross and follow me" (v. 34). This is the first of three predictions of Jesus' suffering and resurrection (8:31; 9:31; 10:33-34), three inappropriate responses by the disciples (8:32-33; 9:32-34; 10:35-41), and three discourses on discipleship (8:34–9:1; 9:35-50; 10:42-45) in the Gospel

of Mark. See the pattern? Prediction of suffering, inappropriate response, and a discourse on discipleship. This was so
important to Mark that he wrote about it three times in three
consecutive chapters. It makes you wonder if his readers
needed to hear this message. In every series of lessons, Mark
ends with what it means to be a follower of Jesus. In every
case, Mark emphasizes that as Jesus followers, we are called
to bear our cross. He does not indicate what the specifics of
that embrace look like. He simply says that's the way it is
supposed to be. In other words, embrace the pain of your
journey.

Intellectually and religiously, I can understand that.
Emotionally and physically, I don't understand, or maybe
I don't want to understand. That's why I love Peter in this
message. I am the Peter type. Are you? If someone tells me
bad things are going to happen, I automatically go into
prevent mode. That will not happen if I have anything to do
with it. I will not let it come to pass. We will organize, set up
some committees, develop some teams, go through strategic
planning processes, work on our priorities and strategies and
tactics, and have a leadership retreat. We will move on and we
will move up, but we will not have this talk of suffering and
pain! That's Peter's plan, isn't it? And it's ours for the most
part, too. I mean, we didn't plan on suffering and pain at our
leadership retreat this past February. It's not something for
which you plan. It's not part of our church growth strategy.
But, sisters and brothers, maybe we were unaware that pain
and suffering are a part—even an integral part—of church
growth. Maybe this road of sorrow makes us grow closer to
each other than ever before. Maybe these tears help us grow
in our dependence on a loving God. Maybe Jesus knew this,
which is why his rebuke of Peter was so harsh: "Get behind
me, Satan!" Have you ever been to a meeting where you
heard someone say this to another person? Can you imagine

how awkward that would be? Peter must have been morti-
fied by being called out like this—by Jesus of all people. The
other disciples were probably wide-eyed and then thankful
that they didn't speak out since they likely felt the same way
Peter did. I'm glad that was Peter and not me!

Jesus knew what Peter could not imagine, and the same
is true for us. Jesus knows what we cannot imagine, so when
Jesus says that we should embrace pain, well, we should
embrace pain. And I want to reiterate what I said last week.
This is not the only way and the final way to respond to pain.
In this instance, this is what Jesus told the disciples. Other
situations will require a different response, as is evidenced in
the fact that we have three more sermons to go! There are
at least three more responses to talk about. Today, we will
embrace pain.

Why embrace pain, and how? There is a connection
between suffering and love. The more you open yourself
up to love, the more vulnerable you are to pain. Examples
abound: when someone you love hurts, you hurt more than
you would if it was a stranger. When you see a stranger in pain,
you take pity or feel bad for them. When you see someone
you love in pain, you cry, you experience empathetic pain, you
suffer, you pray, you ask God why. Few people advocate for
cancer research unless they have been ill or have had a family
member who has suffered with the disease. Our capacity for
pain is almost directly proportional to our capacity to love.
The more you love, the more you open yourself to pain. By
embracing pain, we say that the hurt we experience is worth
it. Jesus says that it is better to experience pain and know love
than to live a pain-free life—at least, that is how I'm inter-
preting Jesus. To this end, we are called to take up our cross.
Bear the pain. Embrace the pain out of the love we have for
God and each other.

That's not all. Embracing pain helps us accept a hard reality. Accepting the reality of Jesus' suffering and death must have been hard for all the disciples, and Peter is the only one who voiced his difficulty—and voiced it loud! Mark says he rebuked Jesus. Peter wanted to deny the truth of the moment. He was unwilling to accept the reality that Jesus proclaimed. This may be why Peter was so dismissive of Jesus when Jesus was arrested. Peter's denial of reality in this passage may have resulted in his more famous denial later in the Gospel. Jesus was trying to prepare Peter for that moment, but Peter wouldn't listen.

We all know too well, especially in this last week, that reality can be hard to accept. We know this because we have learned so much about pain and suffering. It was written across 400 pairs of eyes yesterday. Grief hangs in the air, and today, for now, we will embrace it. We will embrace the pain because it is evidence of our love for someone who is no longer among us. We will also embrace this pain because we need to accept the reality of the moment in order to be healthy now and in the future.

I want to tell a story from this past week that was a turning point for me. It was a God moment if I've ever had one. One morning this week, I sat with Chet and Marcy to plan the funeral service. It seemed appropriate that the recessional should be a guitar solo for Chet. Earlier in the week, Ken McGarry—the youth minister from Wilton Congregational Church—said he would do anything the Burchetts needed if we let him know. Well, he plays the guitar, so Chet and Marcy asked me to contact him to see if he would play this final solo. They told me to let Ken know the kind of music that Chet liked and ask him to play something appropriate— you know, something appropriate from Rancid or The Clash or The Ramones. I left Ken a message about this.

Later that day I went to Starbucks in search of some of Chet's friends because that's where they all would hang out, and sure enough, there was Cody and Antoine and others. I told them to come by my office, and they left their coffee and cigarettes and came. In the middle of the conversation, Cody said, "Jason, I know this is none of my business, but I need to say this. Whenever we were listening to music, there were two songs that, when Chet would hear them, he would always say, 'I want these played at my funeral.'" They were the songs "Radio" by Rancid and "Amazing Grace" by the Dropkick Murphys. I told Cody I'd see what I could do.

A couple of hours later I was on the phone and a call came in. I ignored it, and when I had time I checked my messages. It was Ken McGarry. His message went like this: "Hey, Jason, I'll be more than honored to play at Chet's funeral. I used to be the lead guitar in a punk band, so I'm very familiar with the music. I could play anything—maybe something like 'Amazing Grace' by the Dropkick Murphys. Just let me know." I think that was God saying, "I am right here; I am with you."

Knowing that God is with us in our deepest, darkest moment helps us look up with sober eyes and embrace our pain. Peter's path may resonate with us, but the way of Christ is what leads us home. Amen.

Embracing Pain (A Response)

This was by far the most difficult sermon I had to preach. I had exhausted my energy preparing to preach the funeral sermon the day before and had none left for Sunday's service or for preaching this sermon. When I walked into the sanctuary during the processional, I felt unequipped, unprepared emotionally and mentally to bear the heaviness of the morning. Sitting in front of everyone was painful; I could see their pain and grief, and our collective sadness weighed on my

soul. Still, seeing people I loved going through such misery,
yet still able to pull themselves out of bed, get dressed, and
come to church was profound. I wanted to tell everyone just
to go home and rest and celebrate the strength of their faith.
Then, this sermon—Embracing Pain. It felt feeble; I felt
feeble, but there are times in ministry when you simply have
to get through it. This was one of those times. No running
away, no hiding in an office. Front and center. My leadership
and presence in that moment would be more powerful than
the words, but that very same leadership and presence would
be what gave those words power and efficacy. Maybe every
Sunday should be held with the same weight, but that would
be too overwhelming for even the best ministers. There may
be some consolation in the fact that people don't come to
church to listen to a preacher (or they shouldn't); they come
to experience God. On this morning, I had to leave it up to
God to show up.

The lectionary passage for this Sunday was very difficult
and perfect at the same time. These paradoxes—blessings and
curses—blanketed this entire season of Lent. Even passages
like these were painful and healing. Mark 8:31-38 is where
Jesus predicts his death and tells his disciples to take up their
cross and follow him. It is in this encounter where Jesus
rebukes Peter for trying to prevent it. A passage so blatantly
about life and death was a balm of healing to us the day after
Chet's funeral—and a terrible reminder of what we already
knew.

Peter plays a pivotal role in the passage and in the sermon.
I focus on him in the sermon probably because he responded
to Jesus' prediction in a way that reminds me of myself. It
seems to me that Peter would have gladly accepted his own
cross and followed Jesus. His issue was with Jesus' cross. He
couldn't bear the idea that Jesus would die, much less die on
a cross. It is often easier for us to handle our own pain than

to see someone we love suffer, but we don't get to make that choice. Life happens and we have to deal with what comes our way. Looking out at the people I loved in that church, on that morning after the funeral, was just terrible. It was a Holy Saturday experience more than anything else. We all shared this cross together in communal suffering. We were all Peter. If there was anything we could have done to prevent such a painful death, any of us would have. Unlike Peter in Mark's narrative, we were already past the point of being able to do anything. We shared our collective helplessness through our tears.

Somehow we were supposed to read the text and hear in the sermon some advice on how to embrace pain. Maybe "embrace" is too intimate for a moment. "Accept" may have been a better term, but it was too soon. "Embrace" makes me think of Mary in Michelangelo's *Pietà*, her expression gentle but not anguished as she holds Jesus across her lap. Unlike Mary, our suffering was written clearly on our faces. I think the words of this sermon were received well in part because the congregation knew I was suffering, too. I was not removed from them or their grief. Without that sense of solidarity, I don't think this sermon or any of the sermons in the series would have been received well. Honestly, I don't think I could have done any better than these sermons. At the time, I didn't have the strength.

The connection between love and pain, however, was pertinent. We knew exactly how proportional those two emotions are to each other. There is a deep reciprocity between love and pain. This isn't anecdotal information either; science has shown that the place in the brain that is activated during physical pain is the same region or overlaps significantly with the part of the brain that is activated during social duress. In fact, Eric Jaffe shows that the connection between love and pain is so close that taking pain medication like Tylenol can actually help with a "broken heart."[2] Having a broken heart literally hurts in similar fashion to being hit in the face. However, the effects of emotional pain lasts much longer than physical pain, as Jaffe makes clear, "A kick to the groin might feel just as bad as a breakup in the moment, but while the physical aching goes away, the memory of lost love can linger forever."[3] What's interesting about this research is the fact that love and affection also have healing affects—they can lessen pain. This is why holding a child after they have hurt themselves makes a real difference in their experience of pain, which leads to Jaffe's conclusion: "At least for all the hurt love causes, it has an equally powerful ability to heal."[4] For us, and I knew this then but not in terms of Jeffe's article, our collective suffering, our "holding each other" through this death, had a healing component. Our love for Chet was directly proportional to the pain we were experiencing in his death, but the love we had for each other as a congregation was mediating the pain of that same loss. I cannot imagine trying to go through something like this without a congregation or community of some sort. Unmediated pain in a moment like this would have been simply too much to bear.

The final call to embrace pain in the sermon ends with a story about the coincidence regarding the guitar solo. In the darkest moment of our congregational life, this was a true sign of hope and presence. I cannot say how important something like this is. While that "little miracle" didn't change the situation, it did help us all feel like God hadn't utterly forsaken or forgotten us—maybe I should simply personalize this and say that's what this story did for me. That shimmer of light helped me embrace or accept what was happening.

Acceptance is vitally important in traumatic experiences because it helps one heal, and the sooner you can move toward acceptance the better it will be for your long-term health. In psychotherapy there is a practice called Acceptance and Commitment Therapy (ACT).[5] This therapy helps clients stop denying their problems and moves them toward acceptance with the realization that their feelings of hopelessness and helplessness may be appropriate given their trauma. Suffering, rather than being abnormal, is a normal part of the human experience and therefore shouldn't be treated as an abnormality. Accepting pain is integral to being human and healthy.

Human suffering is inescapable and in that sense it is normal. It is normal to hurt in incomprehensible ways when someone you love dies. If you stay in ministry long enough, you will experience this pain within your congregation. If you stay alive long enough, you will experience this pain in your own life. Nothing can prepare you for a sudden death, and a suicide complicates emotions further. But a minister's capacity to accept the complexities and the pain of humanity will make these moments somewhat less acute—maybe.

In some ways my desire to share this experience with others who may go through something similar is an attempt to help others embrace the inevitable and, in that way, help them prepare. Anyone who has already experienced something as painful as a sudden death or a suicide probably understands that sentiment. The offering here is not so much scientific, however many footnotes I provided to show the science behind the ideas. The offering here is something more sapiential. I hope those who have to face this in their future may be better equipped if they find this book. If it's too late, and you are in the middle of it now, I hope these words embrace your pain—I hope these words embrace you—with love and compassion. Maybe that's how we can embrace pain.

Notes

1. Grander E. Westberg, *Good Grief* (Minneapolis: Fortress Press, 1997), 9.

2. See Eric Jaffe, "Why Love Literally Hurts," *Association for Psychological Science* (February 2013), www.psychologicalscience.org/observer/why-love-literally-hurts.

3. Ibid.

4. Ibid.

5. See Steven C. Hayes, Kirk D. Strosahl, and Kelly G. Wilson, eds., *Acceptance and Commitment Therapy: The Process and Practice of Mindful Change* (2nd ed; New York: The Guilford Press, 2012). In their first chapter, they deal specifically with human suffering—it is the starting point for their work. Within that chapter they discuss suicide, not as an aberration in the human experience, but something more common than we may expect. A more recent publication, specifically for therapists but not too technical, is Jason B. Luoma, Steven C. Hayes, and Robyn D. Walser, eds., *Learning ACT: An Acceptance & Commitment Therapy Skills Training Manual for Therapists* (2nd ed; Oakland, CA: Context Press, 2017).

5

Confronting Pain

John 2:13-22
March 15, 2009
Wilton Baptist Church

"In a conspiracy of silence, one word of truth rings like a pistol shot."[1] This morning we are going to talk about several pistol shots. Poverty issues as words of truth—we don't like to talk about that. But the fact of the matter is that, in the wealthiest country on the face of the planet, 37 percent of our population lives in poverty, and millions more are officially living above the poverty line but are still devastatingly poor. One social theorist has said, "Poverty is not just the problem of those who are poor. Understanding the sources and nature of poverty is in fact the basis for addressing some of the larger social problems of our day."[2] There is nothing glorious about poverty. When children go hungry and people are sleeping in cars and on the streets and there is nothing for them, that's painful—that's pain. *Pistol shot.*

Individual responsibility as words of truth—we like to use this as an excuse to do nothing. Many of us want to put the burden of responsibility on the individual and overlook the systemic problems we have as a society. Although we cannot use this as an excuse to do nothing, this is a truth. As Baptists, we are terribly independent and argue for each individual being responsible for their own lives before God. Everyone has to be responsible for their own actions, even those living in poverty. But before we blame the poor for being poor, listen to this story. In the ancient story, a man sat by the city dump. Though once blessed in many ways, he had nearly lost it all: his health, his wealth, and his children. Such a person was, in the eyes of that age, destitute. Health gave hope for the day's labor. Wealth was power to face the bigger trials. Children meant protection and someone to lean on in the closing years. All were now gone. The situation was difficult for him to comprehend. Nothing in his experience had prepared him for such catastrophes. He had followed the rules. He had been an exemplary, even notable citizen. In his mind he wondered at the extent of the disaster. He could not find a reason for it. As he sat in the pain of his crumbling body, he doubted he could keep his sanity.

Along came three of his friends who had known him in the blessed times. They, too, sat down in consternation. Only, in their case, the difficulty was not pain or hopelessness; rather it was how to make sense of such troubles. They concluded, "God must be angry at you because of your sins for you to suffer so." And that's just what they told him.

From ages ago, we have this story of the troubles of Job. His three friends came to him and offered thoughts that were comforting, that is, comforting to themselves. It is easier to deal with the problems of others in need if you decide that their troubles have been caused by their own willful sin. In that case, you can take part in the "justice" of the situation when you do not help at all. Should you choose to help, even just a little, such magnanimity would show your great virtue. In the eyes of Eliphaz, Bildad, and Zophar, Job had caused his own suffering. But at the conclusion of the book of Job, their counsel was condemned by God. As the world has done since the time of Job, we struggle today with the phenomenon of people in need—sometimes great need. Is it sufficient for God's people to offer no more than the foolish counsel of Job's friends?[3] *Pistol shot.*

In the past, if you were dealing with depression or any type of mental [health] issues, you were supposed to keep it to yourself or keep it in the family. You were not to talk about this pain. This pain was to be suffered in silence—a conspiracy of silence. These family secrets have been absolutely devastating for those suffering with depression and those who watch a loved one suffer. But to be quiet, to keep it to yourself—there is no room for that today. *Pistol shot.*

In each one of these situations of sorrow, we must *confront the pain.* The consequences of leaving these types of pain unattended are like ignoring a gangrenous limb; it will fester and rot until the whole body is sick and ultimately dead. When will our eyes finally tire of seeing children strapped with impoverishment that has been their only inheritance? When will our consciences be pricked until we take people by the hand and lead them from irresponsibility to responsibility? When will we finally get worn out seeing each other battling mental illnesses without ever talking about it? All these questions ask the same thing. What will finally drive us as a Christian community to take action for the most vulnerable in our society and against the evil that opposes them and us?

In our passage today, Jesus turned over the tables in the temple—*pistol shot.* What caused Jesus to "lose it"—or, for the more religious, what caused so much righteous indignation in our Savior? This practice of exchanging money and buying animals for sacrifice was completely accepted during that time, but money changers made a great profit from the exchange. They were taking advantage of pilgrims who had come from all over the world to worship God. This practice prohibited some who had traveled from far away from participating in worship. It happened like this: The "money changers" who are named in this passage would convert foreign currency into the coins allowed in the temple. These temple coins were somewhat sacred and were the only thing that could be used to purchase animals for sacrifice. The money changers acted as the bank that would exchange the currency from all over the Greco-Roman world. These money changers could set the exchange rate at whatever they wanted—there were no regulators back then, either! I know it's hard for us to imagine corruption in banks these days, but that's what it amounted to in this context. The money changers were padding the exchange rate to make a bundle of money. By doing so, they were taking advantage of good religious people who had traveled for days and weeks to make a pilgrimage to Jerusalem and worship the one true God. That's almost as bad as Bernie Madoff![4] It was this type of systemic stealing from faithful people, who only wanted to worship God, that caused Jesus to plat a whip and start taking care of business. He cleansed the den of thieves! *Pistol shot.*

This is the event in the Synoptic Gospels that hastened Jesus' trial before the authorities. In John, it is placed at the beginning of Jesus' ministry to emphasize the division between him and the religious authorities of his day. In both cases, in John and the Synoptic Gospels, this event is intimately related to his crucifixion. So there are two levels of pain in this passage: (1) the injustice happening to the people and (2) the prediction of Jesus' death. On both levels, Jesus absolutely confronts pain—he takes it on. He is neither denying nor embracing pain. He is raging against it! Jesus confronts the pain of injustice and the pain of his own death in this one action. He could not look on this systemic evil and turn the other cheek. And we read in every Gospel account that he knew this would eventually lead to his death. This was the first step to Calvary, and Jesus took it boldly. Jesus confronted pain, and it rang like a pistol shot throughout Jerusalem.

This is typical of any advocacy response to pain and suffering. In fact, without pain and suffering at some level, there would be no need for advocacy. Advocacy is for those who are not able to confront pain on their own for various reasons. It is a collective voice that challenges pain and power. It forces power to move toward alleviating unnecessary pain. This is like the Dr. Seuss story *Horton Hears a Who*. I never knew there was so much social commentary in children's books until I started reading so many of them. Even though the Whos were small, they were people after all. Horton the elephant knew this because he could hear their voices when no one else would listen. Horton would not budge or waver! He confronted the suffering that the Whos were about to face, and he would not relent. In the end, Horton helped the Whos raise their own voices so that everyone could hear them.

How many people in this world are small—too small for us to take notice? What kind of pain do they face every day? Is it the pain of poverty, the pain of irresponsibility, the pain of mental illness? What prohibits them from being able to stand up and speak out? Do they have someone who will stand up and speak out for them? When we look at the world in which we live, are we driven like Jesus to start making plans for change? Are we driven to start turning over tables? Are we driven to action by the pain and suffering all over the place? If we take Jesus as our example for today, we must confront the pain that destabilizes lives and start making a difference in our world. Where there is pain and suffering and sorrow, we are called to make a difference. Confront the pain of poverty. Confront those who by their irresponsibility make their family and friends suffer. Confront the pain in your own life that prohibits you from being fully human. Confront the pain in the lives of your loved ones who are suffering from illness. Intervene! Make a difference. Confront the pain. Do not keep silent. Be a *pistol shot!* Amen.

Confronting Pain (A Response)

I don't know what it was about this sermon in particular, but I remember it very clearly even after more than a decade. It may be that this one was the result of a solid week of contemplation after the funeral. I still cannot believe how unprepared I was the first Sunday after the funeral. That oversight was a mistake I made sure not to repeat, which may be why I remember this sermon so specifically. The paradox is, however, that I remember delivering the sermon but not preparing or writing it. As I try to remember why I wrote what I wrote, I am at a loss. But preaching the sermon and delivering it in the sanctuary that morning are vivid.

I was angry by this point. I wanted to confront something, to shout at something. All of us in the congregation felt like this to a degree, and I am sure therapists could place this feeling in the stages and overlapping layers of grief.[5] The anger felt primal. I could feel Jesus' confrontational emotions when I read this passage in a way that was visceral—and in a way I had never experienced before reading this particular passage.

I did not write this in the sermon all those years ago, but it was part of my meditations on this Scripture. Knowing he was going to die, as is clear from the end of this passage when the narrator of the Fourth Gospel says so, Jesus was at a heightened state of emotion. The week after his death, every-body who knew Chet was stretched thin with exhaustion and pain; it was like we were all waiting for something to explode and did not know what exactly might set it off. Maybe that is what the money changers represent—that final straw at the precise moment when everything is at a breaking point. This sermon on confronting pain functioned that way. It provided all of us a place (maybe even a safe place and in a safe way) to turn some tables over emotionally. I cannot speak for everyone in the congregation, but I certainly needed it.

Anger is one appropriate response to grief. Each of these sermons functions as a response to grief. While our loss was not the primary focus of these sermons, this series of sermons contained my responses to our collective loss. I was dealing with it publicly every Sunday in front of my entire congre-gation. According to The Center for Complicated Grief, "if the loss is permanent, so too is the grief, but its form evolves and changes as a person adapts to the loss."[6] Each sermon was a form of adapting. This one was full of anger with a laser focus on confrontation. Jesus turning over the tables in the Temple gave us the permission we needed to feel what we felt—or at least gave me permission to feel what I felt—and that was anger.

The line from Czesław Miłosz is one of my all-time favor-ites and provides the sermon with a structural backbone—see "*pistol shot*" repeated throughout. While using the passage from the Fourth Gospel as a narrative, this quote provides the structure, and I think the two exegete each other well. I address three "pistol shots" or words of truth that function as a conspiracy of silence. I do not remember why these three in particular were my focus. Stranger still, while I really like how I used the story of Job, it wasn't in the lectionary for that Sunday, so I don't remember how I came to that passage either. In this way, sermons are all pieces of art—some good, some terrible, some transformational, some gross injustices to public speaking. But they are an art form that flows from an individual's mind/heart onto paper or directly into words depending on one's religious tradition. Inspiration is hard to describe and even harder to remember, especially in detail.

Our church, for the most part, would have agreed with these points regarding poverty, individualism, and mental health. In that sense, they were not real "pistol shots" in that congregation at all. We agreed on the theology of these three points, which is why I preached with such veracity—we were collectively turning over the tables in our larger American society. Focusing on poverty, individualism, and mental health seems odd to me now. The first two points certainly go together both in the sermon and in general. Many blame the poor for being poor and dissect people living in poverty to find the problem within them rather than acknowledging the fact that we live in a system that is built to create poverty for the masses and wealth for the few. I wonder if I felt compelled to place mental health with this dyad due to Chet's death. I am certain that was part of it, but I cannot recall exactly how that went.

In hindsight, I should have spent this entire section of the sermon on mental health even though the economic piece directly ties into the passage. The stigma of a mental health diagnosis still prevents people from getting the help they need to function effectively and to feel good. I could have focused on this, which would have been important for the congregation at the time. These are the small regrets we always have as ministers and preachers. Even when we write everything down and read over it and reread it and edit it and prepare, we can always look back and think we should have done something different to make it better. We keep moving forward and learning. Sermons live on in a variety of ways, and a wise minister must trust God and let it go.

At this point in the sermon I begin to deal with the theme of confronting pain and to use the narrative of Jesus cleansing the Temple. It is clear from reading the sermon that my earlier focus on poverty and individualism was based on how I interpreted the money changers in this passage. That connection is important but makes the third point about mental health only more out of place. In any case, Wilton Baptist Church in Wilton, Connecticut, sits in one of the wealthiest counties in the world. Many of the parishioners at the church worked in the financial industry as hedge fund managers, investment bankers, as well as leaders in large corporations. We were full of money changers! The main difference is that most of them did not manage the money of religious organizations— religious organizations were too small! I learned over my life and ministry at Wilton Baptist that money does not exempt one from pain or suffering or loss or grief. None of us could buy our way out of our pain. Our church was full of good people, and we were all suffering a loss too large to comprehend no matter how wealthy we were. We were trying to confront that pain in this sermon.

Life is always complex, and in moments like the one we were facing we realized that all those "normal" complexities did not stop for us to grieve. Our grief was just piled on all the other complexities. There is a desperate feeling of hopelessness and helplessness. And in all truth, sometimes all you can do is mourn. But that mourning can come out in all different forms. After rereading this sermon to craft this response, I feel like this last section is the best part because it connected precisely with our grief at that moment and granted us permission to accept all our various feelings that were coming all at once and overlapping and competing— anger, sadness, even joy when we shared memories of Chet. Jesus' anger gave us comfort around our own.

The final turn toward advocacy at the end and the use
of *Horton Hears a Who* tempered that anger and helped
give it a more useful edge. Horton is certainly not as angry
as the image of Jesus turning over tables, but his compassion and care are what make the Dr. Seuss book so good. A
massive compassionate elephant stands in such contrast to
the infinitesimal voices of the Whos. A children's book versus
the Gospel of John; Horton versus Jesus. Both advocate for
the most vulnerable. One is angry and turning over tables.
One is compassionate and cuddly—begging for his friends.
Both did the same thing in completely different ways. Both
confronted injustice as advocates. Jesus' anger gave us permission; Horton's compassion gave us grace. Honestly, I was glad
for both. We needed to throw some tables around. We also
needed some compassion to take care of ourselves.

Notes

1. Czesław Miłosz, "Nobel Lecture," delivered on December 8, 1980,
www.nobelprize.org/prizes/literature/1980/milosz/lecture/.

2. John Iceland, *Poverty in America: A Handbook* (Berkeley: University
of California Press, 2006), 147.

3. Ruby K. Payne and Bill Ehlig, *What Every Church Member Should
Know about Poverty* (St. Louis, MO: RFT Publishing Co., 1999),
10–11.

4. Bernie Madoff was a financier in New York City who created a
Ponzi scheme that defrauded his investors of nearly $66 billion. In
2009, during the Great Recession, Madoff was sentenced to more than
150 years in prison. Many of his investors lived in and around our
community.

5. While somewhat controversial now, Elizabeth Kübler-Ross first
popularized this notion of the stages of grief in her work *On Death and*

Dying: What the Dying Have to Teach Doctors, Nurses, Clergy and Their Own Families (New York: Macmillan, 1970). A leading expert in grief studies, M. Katherine Shear, has been researching complicated grief for over two decades. She is founding director of The Center for Complicated Grief at Columbia University's School of Social Work. The full resources of the Center can be found at complicatedgrief.columbia.edu/for-the-public/resources/. This website is an invaluable resource for grief in general and has specific resources for suicide.

6. The Center for Complicated Grief, "Key Definitions," complicatedgrief.columbia.edu/professionals/complicated-grief-professionals/overview/.

6

Relieving Pain

John 3:14-21
March 22, 2009
Wilton Baptist Church

> Paint chippin' on cracked walls
> Colors fadin' in narrow halls
> Woman next to me has two half feet
> Injustice of the system can't be beat
> Bad lighting, hard plastic chairs
> The order and progress major cares
> Doctor ate late and then he lied
> It's OK if no one died
> Justice gets better each passing day
> Explain the rich who get a say
> The man before me with one strong leg
> Goes back to the street in the heat to beg.[1]

This poem by our own Gordon Olivea, written while he lived in Brazil, captures something stunning and difficult about the pain and suffering that is all around us. It captures the inevitability of it all—the inescapable aspect of pain and suffering and the hopelessness that accompanies it. In a world where the rich get richer and the poor starve to death, what is our role as Christians? In a world where sorrow runs so deep, how do we respond? In a world where darkness outshines the light, what are we to do? These questions plague us. "The man before me with one strong leg goes back to the street in the heat to beg." What do we do? And how do we make sense of it all when we are the man with one strong leg?

There isn't a single answer to these questions. Christians have been trying to confront the issue of pain for as long as Christianity has existed. It continues to be a problem. It seems at times that our own existence and difficulty with pain contradicts the promises that we find in Scripture. In the Gospel of John, Jesus says he will send a comforter, the Holy Spirit. He also says in the same Gospel, "Take heart; I have overcome the world" (16:33). When we are faced with devastating crises, these words can comfort us or seem incredibly superficial. When our bodies are stricken with incurable illness, what does it mean to say that Jesus is a healer? When we lose a loved one to tragedy, what does it mean to say that Jesus is the resurrection and life? If you think I'm being unfair to our faith, brothers and sisters, know that these are the questions people put to our faith every day. Does our faith come up wanting when these questions are applied? Does our faith fail in times of trial?

In today's passage of Scripture, Jesus is speaking to Nicodemus. By the time we get to our verses, Nicodemus has faded into the darkness from which he came and the dialogue between him and Jesus has become a monologue. Jesus is answering a question Nicodemus posed: "What does it mean to be born again?" (John 3:4, 9). A better translation would be, "What does it mean to be born from above?" You can rephrase this question to capture the answer that Jesus gives Nicodemus: "What does it mean to be a Christian?" At first, this may not seem to have anything to do with the problem of pain, but in fact it's at the heart of the issue. *What does it mean to be a Christian?* Nicodemus asks. Jesus responds with an illustration from the Old Testament: "Just as Moses lifted up the serpent in the wilderness, so must the Son of Man be lifted up" (v. 14). Jesus is referring to a passage in Numbers 21:9. After the children of Israel were liberated from slavery in Egypt and while they were wondering for forty years in the wilderness before coming into the promised land, they were met with all sorts of obstacles. Hunger and thirst are the two most famous complaints they had, and we know the stories of how God dealt with them. When they were starving to death and wanting to return to slavery, God made manna rain down from heaven. When they were thirsty and without water, they remembered the fresh water of the Nile from which they used to drink when they lived in servitude in Egypt. God gave them fresh water from a solid rock in the wilderness. A less popular story is related here. Jesus reminds Nicodemus of the story of Moses responding to a different kind of wilderness suffering. The children of Israel suffered continual run-ins with poisonous snakes; being from Mississippi, I know what that's like! God told Moses to construct a golden serpent, put it on the end of a long pole, and lift it high so that it could be seen throughout the camp of Israelites. Whenever a poisonous snake bit someone, they could look to the golden serpent and be healed. They would live! God gave them water, God gave them food, and God gave them life.

Jesus tells Nicodemus that, just as the serpent was lifted up, so must he be lifted up. Jesus wasn't talking about hymns and praise songs when he said he must be lifted up. Jesus wasn't talking about our prayers when he said he must be lifted up. Jesus wasn't talking about our good deeds when he said he must be lifted up. Jesus was not lifted up by worship, prayers, or service. Jesus was lifted up on a cross! In the following verse, Jesus says, "whoever believes in me shall have eternal life." *What does it mean to be a Christian?* Nicodemus asks. Believe that I died for you, Jesus responds. John 3:16, the next passage, says, "For God so loved the world that he gave his only Son, so that everyone who believes in him may not perish but have eternal life." Listen to the grace of verse 17: "Indeed, God did not send the Son into the world to condemn the world, but in order that the world might be saved through him." Saved, just like the snake-bitten Israelites bound to die a poisonous death. The word used here in verse 17 that is translated as "saved" can also mean "healed" and "rescued." Jesus came not to condemn but to rescue, save, and heal. What does it mean to be a Christian? It means that you are saved, rescued, and healed by Jesus' actions on the cross. What is central to the Christian faith is the cross of Christ—his pain, his suffering, his sorrow. He took our sin away by taking it upon himself, knowing full well that he would suffer the cross for our sins. This is the cost of salvation.

Does our faith fail in times of trial? When posed with the problem of pain, does our faith come up wanting? When you find the cross of Christ at the center of your faith, you know there is a God who understands the excruciating pain of humanity. When you see that Jesus died so we could live, you know there is a God who loves you. We may falter in times of trial—we are human—but the faith that we affirm stands strong.

Jesus knows pain, Jesus knows suffering, and Jesus knows sorrow. Because Jesus loves us, he wants to spare us pain, suffering, and sorrow. He starts with the eternal and moves to the present. He starts with our eternal life and moves to our present circumstances. Our life on earth, no matter how long we live, is short compared to eternity. God knows this better than we do, so God starts with eternity. Through Jesus we have eternal life. Our salvation and ultimate healing are already present with us in a profound way but will only be fully consummated upon our arrival at the pearly gates. Until then, we are caught in this stage of already and not yet. Our salvation is already secure, but we have not yet fully realized the eternal ramifications of that salvation. Until we reach eternity, we will be no strangers to pain. Suffering will knock on our door. Sorrow will barge right on in!

Through the strength we glean from the salvation we have, we will defy pain, we will embrace pain, and we will confront pain, but we will also relieve pain. Because we know, too, what pain feels like, we will reach out to each other and our brothers and sisters who don't come to our church, and we will touch them with the healing hand of a wounded Christ. We will be what Henri Nouwen calls "wounded healers." When one of us hurts, we will surround each other and relieve that pain one day at a time, minute by minute. When someone in our community hurts, we will stand with them and reach out from our own place of pain and offer a healing and helping hand. When our brothers and sisters from around the world only have one good leg and must go back to the street in the heat to beg, we will stand beside them and offer them our legs to stand on, knowing full well that we stand on the rock. How does our faith stand up to the scrutiny of pain and suffering and sorrow? We hurt together! The God of transcendence, the creator God of Genesis, the burning bush, the pillar of fire by night and the cloud by day, the everlasting God, the great I AM descends from the highest heavens, and God hurts with us, too. How do we respond to pain? What's the Christian response to pain? What does it meant to be a Christian? It means that we love God and each

other enough to walk through fire together. We will weather
the storm together, and we will come out on the other end
where there is relief indeed.

Two days after Gordon wrote his poem "One Strong
Leg," he wrote another poem, "Brazilian Sunset."

> Walking through the tunnel of tropical trees
> On rain softened dirt of the path in the breeze
> Embracing my body with pure life flowing free
> Feeling sensuous and lush with God's grace filling me
> Dramatic clouds race and roll for the sky
> Blues and golden hues dance for the eye
> Falling fast the sun shoots its final rays
> I'll hold this memory till the end of my days[2]

Amen.

Relieving Pain (A Response)

In every wedding that I have ever officiated—dozens at this
point in my career—there is a sentence I always include even
when it sounds clichéd. I did not come up with this statement and I do not know where I ever heard it, but the truth
to me is undeniable: "A joy shared is a joy doubled; a sorrow
shared is a sorrow halved." To summarize in the extreme, this
sermon is completely captured in that one sentence. Since
I have not met a preacher that can get away with having
one-sentence sermons, more always must be added.

It's important to emphasize that the doubling and halving
of joy and sorrow only happen in relationship—specifically
in a marriage relationship for the purposes of wedding cere-
monies, but the idea holds for community as well. There is
a sacredness about humanity when we voluntarily commit
to community—to each other. There is tension between
individualism and community, but the one can always

enhance the other when both are healthy. There may be some self-preservation in community, too. Human beings are herd animals and need social groups. Throughout human evolution, our capacity to socialize into larger groups has increased to the extent that cosmopolitans and metropolises are not just possible but successful. Individuals live longer and lead healthier lives if they are in a community of some sort. This has been true as far back as human beings have been studied. In that sense and simply put, we need each other.

Yuval Noah Harari's popular book *Sapiens: A Brief History of Humankind* provides an in-depth look at our social nature from the evolutionary beginning of humanity to the present. The section on the unification of humankind speaks to our continual move toward unity, but shows the violence explicit in the move—violence like colonialism and imperialism as a means toward unification.[3] While this violence is profoundly true about our shared humanity, there is another truth to our shared existence. We are better together, not from coercive means but from cooperative agreement. When I am in community with others, especially with those different from me, I am better than I normally would be. Their difference helps me see the world more holistically; my difference reciprocally helps them.

This is how I understand the nature of this sermon. The opening question goes back to the original question of the entire sermon series: How do Christians respond to pain? The question is nuanced here: How does our Christian faith stand up to the scrutiny of human suffering? Rather than focusing on the actual title of the sermon, "Relieving Pain," I mostly deal with the question of theodicy all over again but begin to grapple with the question that was posed by James L. Crenshaw earlier regarding anthropodicy.

Gordon Olivea's poems create bookends around the sermon. The first looks unflinchingly at human suffering.

This is the starting place. The second looks at the exquisite beauty of nature and speaks to the healing properties of natural beauty. These poems provide a movement from suffering to resolve or relief. The opening poem leaves the question of human pain hanging in your mind with its imagery of people with visible physical disabilities. It prompts the question *Does our Christian faith measure up to pain?* I take that question into the narrative of the Nicodemus story from John 3:14-21 where Nicodemus asks his own questions about eternal life and being born from above or born again.

Jesus' answer to Nicodemus places suffering at the center of his narrative and compares his own eventual death to the suffering of the Hebrews as they wandered in the wilderness with Moses. We absolutely felt lost in the wilderness by the time this sermon came along in Lent. It had been two weeks of suffering and mourning. We identified with the thirst and hunger and the feeling of death that these wandering Hebrews felt in the narrative of Numbers. We needed to look up and find healing and salvation and rescue from somewhere. The solidarity between our experience of suffering and theirs was palpable in our sanctuary that morning. I will never forget how it felt to preach these words about Moses and the wandering—and look out at our congregation and see we were all there in the desert together, thirsty, hungry, and in pain.

In that moment of solidarity in suffering, what we found—and what we knew all along—was Jesus on the cross in the most familiar verse in Baptist life: John 3:16. Love and death so intricately intertwined at the center of our beliefs as Christians. It was a foreshadowing of Good Friday that we had not fully experienced at that point in Lent in spite of our focus on pain throughout the season. There was something mystical about that moment that caused us to all pause and take it in. A suffering God. A suffering people.

At this point, I returned to the question about whether Christian faith measures up to pain and suffering. My great regret here is not spending the rest of my time on the practical implications of a suffering God for a suffering people. We were standing at the edge of that theological mountain, but I switched focus to the eschatological. While the text clearly speaks of eternal life in the crowning verses of this passage (vv. 16-17), I feel like we should have held on to the mystical moment and hovered over the edge of a suffering God. Both the Christian concept of a suffering God and eschatology are answers to the problem of theodicy. They are not mutually exclusive, but they also are not theologically tied closely together. And, there is no reason to move toward the eschatological when dealing with the terminology of "eternal life," but that is what I did here.

It may have been taking the textual cue to use "eternal life" to go toward eschatology, but it also may have been a lazy move. Preaching about the consummation of salvation in the great hereafter is something most Baptists are raised on. We can talk about the end times and our heavenly home like we can talk about a sunrise and rain—something we experience nearly every Sunday in church. I will not deny that I may have been lazy here; at this point, I was so tired my body hurt. These sermons were taking as much life out of me as they were giving life to anybody—at least that is how I felt. Writing these sermons in the midst of trauma felt like secondary trauma every time I looked at the lectionary texts and the sermon titles. In that state, I went with what was easy instead of leading us into the domain of a suffering God.

The already/not yet of our faith, however, is still a powerful tool to talk about our pain and suffering. It is much simpler to understand and can be beneficial when a congregation is already exhausted. There is already something deeply transformative about our Christian faith. The eternal part of eternal life is not all about the life after this one. We are shaped by our faith now, but that is no escape from our current human predicament. The "not yet" of our faith awaits us in that future where there are no tears. That future utopia is a powerful vision that can guide Christians through profoundly painful moments and can call Christians to action that makes the vision more of a reality in the "already." After using this eschatological argument to address theodicy, I come back to the suffering God, which implicitly brings the sermon closest to its title of "Relieving Pain."

Returning to the phrase in Gordon's poem, "one good leg," I put our suffering together with the suffering around the world: "We hurt together." The Burchetts were suffering the loss of a son and brother, and we were suffering with them. I cannot say that this shared suffering halved anyone's suffering. The Burchetts suffered the most. The suffering rippled out from there to the rest of the family, to Chet's friends, to our church, and to the larger religious community, which turned into a remarkable show of love and compassion. Our local rabbi and close friend, Leah Cohen, offered to have several of her congregants from Temple B'nai Chaim stay in our church while we went to the graveside for the funeral service. While we literally buried our loved one, the members of the synagogue were at our church taking down all the chairs in the fellowship hall and keeping an eye on our property. Just writing that makes my eyes tear, and these tears speak to the pain of that moment and the unbelievable love from sisters and brothers who came to suffer with us—who felt our pain and responded as people of faith and human compassion. This is exactly the answer to Crenshaw's question of anthropodicy. And this is the most profound answer to the question of theodicy. We hurt together. God hurts with us.

The title of the sermon, "Relief," may not be the right word, but I do not know a better one. Knowing that you are loved and cared for during a terrible experience is truly a relief. It is not a relief from the pain; it is a relief that you are not alone in it. The love we feel from those who come to our aid when we are suffering tempers our pain. Paradoxically, the love that produces our pain in loss, also gives us the strength to move through that same pain. "Relief" may be the right word after all.

Notes

1. Gordon Olivea, "One Strong Leg," written June 2, 1998. Used with permission.

2. Gordon Olivea, "Brazilian Sunset," written June 4, 1998. Used with permission.

3. Yuval Noah Harari, *Sapiens: A Brief History of Humankind* (New York: Harper Collins Publishing, 2015), 163–246.

7

Redeeming Pain

John 12:20-33
March 29, 2009
Wilton Baptist Church

"How ironic that the difficult times we fear might ruin us are the very ones that can break us open and help us blossom into who we were meant to be."[1] Isn't that a stupid sentence? In what has actually been a great read so far, this is how Elizabeth Lesser begins her most recent book *Broken Open: How Difficult Times Can Help Us Grow*. When I read that sentence, having gone through what we have all be going through this month, I underlined it and wrote in the margins: STUPID! It just seemed like a sentence that was too easy to say yet incredibly hard to accept and believe and live out, especially when you are walking through the fire. I picked up this book because the subtitle *How Difficult Times Can Help Us Grow* seemed to be relevant for a sermon about redeeming pain. Is there any redemption in human suffering? Is there anything good about the pain and sorrow we face as human beings? The answer to this question directly impacts the question with which we've been wrestling throughout Lent, which is *How do we as Christians respond to pain?* I'm glad I didn't throw away Lesser's book after reading that stupid sentence because what I found later has been really helpful personally and professionally. The book is a compilation of real life stories written by sojourners who have traveled the terribly difficult path from the dark night of the soul to living again. The third sentence after that stupid sentence made sense to me, "I share these personal tales because I know that the arc of one triumphant human story traces the potential of each of our lives."[2] Preach it, sister! Lesser says, "I share these personal tales because I know that the arc of one triumphant human story traces the potential of each of our lives." Yes! Yes, indeed. We need to hear some stories of folks who made it. We need to hear the stories of people who have faced down devastation and have come out on the other end. We need to hear these stories so that we can believe that coming out on the other end is possible. Or, at least I need to hear them. So, that "stupid" sentence, let's hear it again: "How ironic that the difficult times we fear might ruin us are the very ones that can break us open and help us blossom into who we were meant to be." Well, maybe there is redemption, even for that sentence. And if it can be redeemed, then maybe our pain can be redeemed as well.

Our passage this morning is a little obscure. It starts with Greeks wanting to see Jesus—we don't know why or what they wanted and they fade as fast as they appeared. This, for some reason, prompts Jesus to begin teaching his disciples. But then the lesson! "Very truly, I tell you, unless a grain of wheat falls into the earth and dies, it remains just a single grain; but if it dies, it bears much fruit. Those who love their life lose it, and those who hate their life in this world will keep it for eternal life. Whoever serves me, the Father will honor. Now my soul is troubled. And what should I say, 'Father, save me from this hour?' No, it is for this reason that I have come to this hour. Father, glorify your name" (John 12:24-28a). It is hard to miss the pain in Jesus' voice in this passage. That's the way pain and sorrow work. Something as random as some Greeks coming to visit hits Jesus just right. When you are dealing with pain, sometimes it just hits you and you have to cry or talk or do whatever you have to do. These Greeks show up and it must just get to Jesus like a trigger. And it prompts him to teach like this. I wonder if his disciples were totally confused? I wonder what the Greeks thought about if they heard Jesus? I don't know, but it seems as though the sorrow of the moment caught Jesus off guard and he gave this teaching. You can hear Jesus coming to terms with his own death. You wonder if he's teaching the disciples or whether or not he's convincing himself of what he has to do. What good is a grain of wheat unless it goes into the ground and dies so that it can produce much fruit? What good is my life if I hold on to it and don't surrender to God's will? Now my soul is troubled. And what should I say— "Father, save me from this hour?" No, it is for this reason that I have come to this hour. Father, glorify your name.

Pain, sorrow, suffering, and then, resolve. Father, glorify your name. My life will redeem all of humanity. Jesus knew that his pain, his cross, would redeem every living human being the planet has ever known. This pain was redeemed because Jesus made a choice. He chose the right thing. I wonder how quiet heaven was when Jesus was trying to get through this moment of decision? I suppose it was quiet. Then Jesus reaches his resolve and says, "Father, glorify your name." What happens next? A voice comes from heaven, "I have glorified it, and I will glorify it again" (v. 28b). It seems that God almighty could not keep quiet any longer after his son had made this decision. Can you hear it in God's voice there? Can you hear the mixture of pain and pride? Knowing what Jesus had just consented to, God had just saved his creation but only at the cost of his son. As any good, loving father would, he couldn't keep quiet. You've just glorified it, son! You did it!

Is there redemption in pain? Can anything good come out of human suffering? The only thing redemptive about pain is what we do with it! Being Christians shapes the "what we do with it" part, or at least it can and it should. We can face our pain with the knowledge that there have been some spiritual and biblical giants that have gone before us, and, as Lesser put it, "I know that the arc of one triumphant human story traces the potential of each of our lives." We see Jesus here making the choice for universal life. He is our guide! He is our example! In the midst of our pain, we look to Jesus and find one who has suffered and died and one who is suffering with us and knows how to console us. And if there is any way out of this mess, it will be because we make the choice and follow his lead. If there is any light at the end of the tunnel, it will be him. If there is any redemption in human suffering, we will only know it because we will have chosen to keep our eyes on the only one who is able to give abundant and eternal life. Instead of retreating and running away from his pain, Jesus chose hope for humanity rather than release from his responsibility. Jesus chose to give us hope. It is our hope in Christ that will see us through our time of trial. And as we walk with Christ into his hope that is higher than our pile of problems, we will be transformed. We will come out different in ways that we would not have thought. We will have grown and gained the capacity to help others in a way that we could not before. We will have become Christians in all the depth that Christian can mean. We will be able to see clearer, love deeper, and hold tighter because we will have come to know ourselves and know the God who loves us. So, does the end of trials justify the means? No. It doesn't justify our pain, but it has the capacity to redeem it, if we will only choose for it to be redemptive. Some don't. I hope we will.

Let me end with a story that Elizabeth Lesser has in her book about Glen. Glen and his wife, Connie, lost Eric, one of their twins sons, to an automobile accident in his early twenties. Here are Glen's words:

> At one point in history, mankind believed that the world was a flat table, and that those foolhardy enough to venture too near the edge would fall off into a terrible world of fierce sea monsters and destruction upon the rocks. They were right. Eric's death pitched us headlong off our daily plane of existence into the darkness to be wrecked upon the rocks. For weeks and months, we roiled and thrashed in pain, submerged in agony, not sensing the light or knowing in what direction to turn. We fought to hang on to each other. Lifelines tossed to us from above were not recognized or were purposefully ignored. Each of us prayed at times to simply drown and be done with it. Were it not for friends and family—who flung themselves into our brokenness, to hold our heads above the water— we may well have drowned in our sorrow. This place of hopelessness and fear is real, not a cute little allegory. Some people never leave that place and are broken on the rocks. Some people stop fighting and slip into the depths. We came to understand that, although we do not have control, we do have choice. God . . . wants us to go down into the dark waters, but also wants us to come up to the light. God will not force us to do so. We are free. We are made so, and it is our great gift. We can choose darkness, fear, addiction, and despair. We can choose light, hope, meaning, and joy. By the grace of God, I chose life.[3]

Does that story redeem pain? Does that story provide an arc of one triumphant human story that can trace the potential for each of our lives? It can if we can find it in ourselves to look at it that way—to choose for it to be redemptive. When it's all said and done, we see that Jesus made a choice. So, answering the question whether pain can be redeemed is tricky. There are two answers: Yes and No. Which will we choose? As we gather around the table of remembrance, ritualizing the redemption that comes through Christ, allow that question to marinate. I ask the Deacons to join me at the table.

Redeeming Pain (A Response, But Different)

What follows is not like the rest of my responses. When I was preparing this book for publication, two things happened. First, the computer that held all of these sermons died, and I did not have them backed up on an external hard drive or in the cloud. As you can imagine, this loss was devastating, primarily because the sermons are a record of my journey through this experience. Thankfully, I had printed a copy of the entire manuscript . . . except the second thing that happened was that I lost that printed copy. Before I lost that version, I had made a back-up copy of everything except this sermon, "Redeeming Pain," so I had truly lost this sermon. I contacted Wilton Baptist Church to see if there was a digital recording of the sermon. There was not. It was gone. With no hope of finding this last sermon and no real recollection of it other than the title, I re-wrote it, and that version is what is below.

Then, after re-writing this sermon, I found the original printed copy in a package I had mailed myself from Washington, DC, because I didn't want to carry so many papers with me on an international trip I was about to take. When I compared them, the two sermons were strikingly similar—down to identical quotes from a common source and how I reacted to both of them.

The opening of the second sermon reflects a decade of thought, not just a month. That intervening decade is what made the meaning of the second sermon possible. In the original sermon, I had to start with someone else's voice (Lesser's voice) just to find my own. That is a major difference between these two sermons: acute grief vs. historical grief. There is a gulf between the two that is only bridged by time.

In the original sermon, I was simply trying to find a way forward, a trace left by someone that I could follow, as the second quote from Lesser's book says. I was still looking for this in the first sermon. Only a month away from this tragic event, I did not have my emotional legs under me. The second sermon is evidence that I found a trace in the collective grief of my sisters and brothers of all faiths—and even no faith. They were there for me. Now I am with them, awaiting other grieving souls who seek the strength of our community of grief.

The original sermon was written by a grieving sojourner looking for a way forward. The second sermon was written by a gentle guide—one who knew the pain of the journey. Both provide an arc to the life of this book. Completing the second sermon and completing the overarching scope of this book give some kind of meaning and purpose to our pain. In other words, if there is any real redemption, then it is a redemption we have consciously chosen—a redemption of our own making. Both sermons speak to this. Redemption is a choice. We choose to move forward or not. The second sermon reveals the decisions I made to move forward with the hope of helping others—those sitting in the pews and those reading these words.

The sermons move toward the biblical text at about the same time, but the way I handle the text in the two sermons indicates my timeline with grief. In the original, I am still experiencing those random, severe stabs of grief—like the Greeks coming to visit Jesus causing him to begin his teaching. In the second sermon, I focus on Jesus' resolve. The resolve comes later in the original sermon and comes as a hope—a hope that resolve may be possible, redemption possible—maybe. The second sermon moves right past Jesus' personal grief to a grief for others. Here, there is a lingering grief that lives more in memory than in the present.

Both sermons end with Glen's story. The original sermon ends with the hope that we choose redemption. But that was a real hope—and I did not even know if I could—so it hangs in the air, a hope to be realized or not. The second sermon encourages the congregation/the readers to keep moving forward, one step at a time. A decade later, I knew it was possible. Taken together, the two sermons are evidence of the arc of grief and healing.

Redeeming Pain 2.0

It has nearly been a month since Chet died and we are still deep in our grief and pain. I still feel lost and I know we all feel that way as the waves of grief come and go in and out of our bodies and minds like the tide. And here we are at the end of this Lenten season, still plugging away at a sermon series on pain and how we respond to it as Christians. I'm not sure if Christians have a different way to respond to grief because it is such a universal human experience. Like other faiths—Judaism, Islam, Hinduism, Buddhism, etc.—we have developed our own specific religious way to respond to a universal experience, and that response is our story and helps us find our way forward with God and each other. But, to be honest, I'm looking to all my religious and non-religious friends for help on this one! Sometimes our grief and pain can feel more powerful than our own faith. Like the pain crushes everything, and nothing can stand up to the power of pain that washes over you and pulls tears out of your eyes and moans out of your lungs.

The reason we decided to focus on our pain is because Lent lends itself to that sort of self-reflection and introspection. It is our season of Lent where we confess and let go of our sins and burdens that hold us down and hold us back. Obviously, pain and grief have a remarkable capacity to do that very thing. This important season compels us to think about our lives and all the many parts that make up our lives—even the deaths in our lives—and try to make some sort of sense about it all. And our Scriptures assigned to us by the lectionary do just that. They are our guide through this journey inward that help us plot our next step and move us toward something that feels so far away right now—the Resurrection.

And what do we find in our Gospel passage for today? Jesus predicting his own death and accepting that pain as a way to glorify God: "Now my soul is troubled. And what should I say—'Father save me from this hour?' No, it is for this reason that I have come to this hour. Father, glorify your name" (John 12:27-28a). Accepting the truth of his reality and the reality of his own death was not something easy for Jesus—"Now, my soul is troubled." It shows us both the pain and resolve that Jesus had at one of the most critical junctures in his life.

His grief regarding his own death wasn't the only thing that was troubling his soul. It surely must have been the first part of this passage that also weighed on Jesus' soul: "Those who love their life lose it, and those who hate their life in this world will keep it for eternal life. Whoever serves me must follow me, and where I am, there will my servant be also" (vv. 25-26a). It wasn't just Jesus' own death that he was mourning; it was the deaths of those who would follow him all the way past his cross to their own. However painful, this was the path to God for Jesus and all those who would follow him then and now. The path to God is through the cross. The cross is not simply the symbol of Jesus' death. The cross is the violent symbol of how this world operates. When forces of good begin to transform the status quo, it is the status quo that strikes back violently. The cross shows how terribly violently the world resists transformation toward what is good and right and peaceful for all. And it stands as a judgment against the world that their violence is not the answer. It is actually in the violent act against what is good that the world is laid bare for all to see.

This is exactly the impetus for the non-violence of the civil rights movement. The violence they endured—even to death—showed the entire world how corrupt and immoral Jim Crow laws were. It was the Christian faith of the civil rights movement that pitted non-violence against violence and the contrast was so stark that it pricked the consciousness not just of America but the whole world. Their pain was like that of Christ in this passage for today. Their souls were troubled, for sure, but what were they to say? It was their self-sacrifice through non-violent direct action that changed the country. This is how their pain was redeemed; this is how the world—the whole cosmos—is saved. Margaret Farley, a powerful voice of love and transformation, says it best in regard to Jesus' acceptance of his own death at the hands of violent evil-doers: "No matter what the forces of evil will do to Jesus, they will not take from his heart his love for God. The 'hour' of utter self-abandonment, and acceptance even of abandonment by God—the hour of love that holds 'no matter what'—is consummation. A human Yes, forever sealed in death, meets the divine Yes, and neither will be revoked."[4]

How do we, in our day-to-day lives, find this power, especially in moments like we are in now in the wake of a tragic death? How does Jesus' cross, and the crosses borne by so many of his followers throughout millennia, shape the way we experience common and complicated grief and pain? Elizabeth Lesser, a spiritual guide of sorts and bestselling author opened her book *Broken Open: How Difficult Times Can Help Us Grow*, with these words of wisdom: "How ironic that the difficult times we fear might ruin us are the very ones that can break us open and help us blossom into who we were meant to be." If you go to my office and pick that book up off my desk and open it to the first page of the introduction, you will see that I underlined that quote. It was the second sentence of the book and the first sentence I underlined. You will also see that I drew an arrow in the right margin that pointed to one word that I wrote in that same margin. I wrote: "stupid." That's right! That was my first reaction to reading her second sentence. You would think that I would have put that book down and never returned. Thankfully I kept reading and found that her opening remarks were not based on some superficial understanding of human pain and suffering, but based on her own personal experiences of loss and twenty-five years of working with people from all over the world who are also dealing with transition and loss.

One of her stories in the book is about Glen. Glen was wildly successful in his career, happy in his marriage, and had three great kids. Eric, one of his twin sons, spent an undergraduate semester abroad at the University of Melbourne in Australia. After his adventurous semester in Australia, he went to New Zealand for three weeks, then planned to return home. On this trip Eric died in a car wreck. As we all know, everyone in the family was inextricably changed. Here's Glen in his own words:

Were it not for friends and family—who flung them-selves into our brokenness, to hold our heads above the water—we may well have drowned in our sorrow. This place of hopelessness and fear is real, not a cute little alle-gory. Some people never leave that place and are broken on the rocks. Some people stop fighting and slip into the depths. We came to understand that, although we do not have control, we do have choice. God or Spirit or Creator or Insert Name Here wants us to go down into the dark waters, but also wants us to come up to the light. God will not force us to do so. We are free. We are made so, and it is our great gift. We can choose darkness, fear, addiction, and despair. We can choose light, hope, meaning, and joy. By the grace of God, I chose life.

Glen closes his story with these words: "Eric is always near. We see him in nature: birds, butterflies, rainbows, and sunsets. But mostly we feel him. We are, each of us, Spiritual Warriors. We are awake, and nothing can break our circle. Nothing will ever be the same again."

We know the power of Glen's last sentence: "Nothing will ever be the same again." But it is in these real human stories—stories from those who have already made the path we are on now because they have traveled ahead of us—that help us move one step at a time forward toward redemption. Their stories of heartache and devastation—like Jesus' own soul-troubling words—give us a path forward. Their pain is redeemed in the way that it helps us forward, and our pain is redeemed not so much for ourselves as for those who come after us. Like the leaders of the civil rights movement, our pain and suffering are only redeemed by the fact that they chart a course for a better world for those who will come later. Our souls are troubled right now. The pain and grief is overwhelming. But as we keep putting one foot in front of the other, holding each other up from falling down, carrying our crosses, and sharing each other's burdens, our pain becomes a pathway toward hope—even if we can't see it yet. Even when we find ourselves in the liminal space between cross and grave, we keep going because there just may be a resurrection somewhere. Maybe even next week. May it be so. Amen.

Notes

1. Elizabeth Lesser, *Broken Open: How Difficult Times Can Help Us Grow* (New York: Villard, 2005), xix.

2. Ibid., 83.

3. Ibid., 85.

4. Margaret A. Farley, "Theological Perspective: John 12:20-33" in *Feasting on the Word: Preaching the Revised Common Lectionary*, David L. Bartlett and Barbara Brown Taylor, eds. (Year B, Volume 2; Louisville: Westminster John Knox Press, 2008), 144.

8

Faded Flowers

Faded flowers on a hill, a tragedy six feet deep.
All that's left are your pictures, songs and memory.
Topsoil leveled on the ground,
It's been a while since you've been around.
Crows are calling, I have to go
But as I do you have to know
That cloudy days and sunshine
Both conspire to remind me of you.
Coming here is getting old—
At least that's what I've been told.
You're not here, but there you are
Calling me from afar.
So, one last lesson don't forget
You are loved without regret!
I remember you, I'll remember you.

The months that followed Chet's death were profoundly difficult for all of us—his parents, of course, suffered the most. I would go to his graveside every day. I'd park my car beside his grave, which isn't far from the little cemetery road. There was also a bench at the bottom of the small hill where he is buried, and I'd go sit there and look up the hill at his tombstone. Most of the time, I stood at the foot of his grave. In these moments, I was keenly aware of my surroundings. I found myself looking for anything that helped me connect to Chet. That's where this poem that follows originated. I watched everyday as the flowers on his grave slowly faded and the groundskeeper finally removed them. The enormous tragedy of his death was acute every time a simple change happened like this. I don't know why taking those faded flowers off his grave hurt so intensely.

That is probably the nature of grief—the unexpectedness of acute moments and inexplicable small things that derail you for a moment. Well over a year after Chet died, I was driving down the road and a song came on the radio that I had never heard before. I immediately liked the rhythm and for some reason it made the think of Chet—probably sounded like the music he used to play when he was in his high school band. For a brief second, I thought, "I can't wait to see him and tell him about this song." As soon as the thought came to my mind, I caught myself. How could I forget he was dead? I felt angry with myself. And then I started missing him in a way I had not for a while, and tears rolled down my cheeks—all the way down my neck.

Years later, memories and tears are the evidence of love and grief. While everyone's grief is different, it is a profound human equalizer. Jesmyn Ward, a great Mississippi author, wrote a memoir, *Men We Reaped*, about her grief of losing five young black men in her life, including her brother. So much of her grief has to do with the loss of these young men, but the added injustices perpetuated against African Americans is a heavy, inextricable layer to her grief. As she writes the stories of these young men, who are deeply part of her own story of love and loss, she says, "But this grief, for all its awful weight, insists that he matters."[1]

Our grief insists that the departed matter long after they are gone. This poem carries my grief and acts as a reminder of all those moments standing in front of Chet's grave—from the graveside service until I finally wrote the words on paper.

The graveside service was as heartbreaking as the funeral itself. Hundreds of people crowded around his grave. I read Scripture and offered a closing prayer. Then, I dismissed everyone—but nobody left. Most of the crowd were teenagers or kids just bursting into their twenties. Chet's family were Texans, so in true Texas fashion, they had family bring Texas soil to the funeral. Everyone waited for Chet's casket to be lowered into the grave; his father took the Texas soil and told everyone that his son was born on Texas soil and would be buried beneath it. Then they opened the container with the soil and poured it onto Chet's coffin. I'll never forget the sound as it landed on Chet's pecan wood casket. That sound echoed in my mind and is the nature of the "tragedy six feet deep."

Before I was the pastor at Wilton Baptist Church, I was the associate pastor, which meant a large part of my job was planning events for the youth. Chet was a central figure in the youth group. One part of planning and organizing an event calendar for youth for over half a decade is making sure we had pictures of the events. When I took a new job in Dallas, Texas, at another church, a good friend at our church framed a picture of the youth group for me as a departing gift. That photograph, with Chet sitting on the church's playground slide with his guitar, still hangs in my house. I was only gone for a year before I came back—and Chet played a central role in that return.

Another favorite picture from my time as their youth minister was taken at a pool party. The kids always wanted to wrestle me in the pool. I was out of the pool getting a snack when Chet tried to grab me and throw me in the pool. He was never really big, and I am build like a tree stump, so his attempt was pretty funny. I grabbed him by his swim trunks and picked him up, giving him a wedgie. Then I put his feet on the side of the pool and leaned him over the water in a way that suspended him in the air. Someone took a picture at this moment. Both of us were looking at the camera with absolute hilarity in our eyes. It was fun. This was the picture and memory in the poem.

The song was all of his songs and music and budding music career all wrapped into one word. Chet's band played at school talent shows and later at local teen centers that were common in lower Fairfield County. One of his first shows was in middle school at a talent show. They had a punk sound and a punk look! He loved his music and was an incredible guitar player. Sometimes I would pick him up from his guitar lessons and take him home. While his mom didn't care too much for the punk look, his parents were wildly supportive of his love for music. On one occasion, his dad took him to a B.B. King concert where Chet got to meet the King of Blues backstage and B.B. King gave him a guitar pick. On the day of the funeral, when the funeral home delivered Chet's body to the church, I put this same guitar pick into his casket. It was my last interaction with Chet, and I was the last person to see him when they closed the casket.

The days after his burial, I slowly watched the mounded dirt on his grave sink to the same height as the ground surrounding his grave. As the topsoil leveled, so did our lives. The whole world had changed in Chet's death, but nothing stopped. Mondays followed Sundays and I had to write a sermon every week after his death just like before. I went into work, kids went to school, day followed night, and our routines continued. It was a paradox that was hard to reconcile. But that soil leveled out and grass started to grow. I marveled at nature's capacity to move forward, incorporate, and regenerate. That leveling topsoil represented my hope for a way forward and offered a model for my own life. And in the same way, its settling and leveling represented the time that had been passing.

Crows are common in Connecticut and they do not migrate through in any given season, so it is not unusual to see crows year-round. However, every time I went to Chet's grave in the months after his death, crows seemed to be there, keeping me company and squawking. The cold, brittle air of Spring in the Northeast was punctuated by their calls, and they were the perfect voice—melancholy, gray. It would have been off-putting to hear some pretty songbird. No matter the weather, the crows had it right.

Sometimes I could stay for a while. Other times I never got out of my car—just stopped for a minute to be there. No matter how long I stayed, I always felt guilty about leaving. I almost always talked to Chet out loud and directly, and just as often I would tell him "I have to go." It was always an apology born out of regret and pain and the desire to let him know that I thought of him every day. I wanted him to know that "cloudy days and sunshine both conspire to remind me of you," and they did.

Months later I was talking to a group of Chet's friends. They would congregate, often smoking, in the outside sitting area of Starbucks—tattoos, ear spacers, brightly dyed hair, metal-spiked belts and bracelets, fringed jeans. I loved these kids, too. I loved their rebellion, loved their cause (even if they did not know what it was), and loved their spirit—partly because they were the outsiders and because others in our otherwise conventional town probably disparaged them. I'd like to think they appreciated that a Baptist pastor liked them so much for who they were. I would get a coffee and sit with them and listen. One of them asked me if it would eventually "get old" to keep going to his grave. I could hear in her voice that part of her wanted to be set free from her grief and the other part that perhaps feared forgetting. I knew what she meant, but I didn't have an answer. It was my question, too—a question that always tinged with a little guilt.

Nearly every time I stood in front of his grave, I had the paradoxical feeling that Chet was both there and not there. Chet's grave was like a picture of him. It represented both his presence and his absence. Going to his grave and reading his tombstone and seeing one of his tattoos engraved in the headstone made me feel close to him—as if he was there. In the same time and in the same way they were all evidence of his absence and confirmed that he was not there. While I wrestled with this every time I came to visit him, I left— mostly—with a sense of his presence. This became more and more true. It was as if his voice became clearer the more I went, and after many months, I could laugh with him there about some of his old shenanigans—not just remembering him but remembering with him.

One of the most pertinent moments for me during Chet's funeral service was when his former high school Sunday school teacher stood up to read Scripture. Jim Stockfisch was not just another Sunday school teacher—he was cool! He was an athlete in his younger years and maintained his physique through his professional life as a construction contractor. He also coached and then refereed lacrosse games throughout the county. Jim had calloused hands and an authentic and perpetual tan even through the long winters of New England. But Jim's heart has no callouses whatsoever—he is honest and genuine to his core. Jim stood to read Romans 8:35-39. He prefaced his reading with: "One last lesson, Chet." Fighting tears, Jim read,

> Who will separate us from the love of Christ? Will hardship, or distress, or persecution, or famine, or nakedness, or peril, or sword? As it is written, "For your sake we are being killed all day long; we are accounted as sheep to be slaughtered." No, in all these things we are more than conquerors through him who loved us. For I am convinced that neither death, nor life, nor angels, nor rulers, nor things present, nor things to come, nor powers, nor height, nor depth, nor anything else in all creation, will be able to separate us from the love of God in Christ Jesus our Lord.

The inseparable love of God was Chet's Sunday school teacher's last lesson. In a true sense, it is the only lesson—one we must not forget.

I loved Chet. I think he knew that. The depth of my grief was worth the love, and, as Jesmyn Ward said, it was proof his life mattered. His life matters still.

Note

1. Jesmyn Ward, *Men We Reaped: A Memoir* (New York: Bloomsbury, 2013), 243.

9

Constructive Aftermath

In the aftermath of Chet's death, his family wanted to create a way to make his memory last, so we worked with them to create a short-term memorial fund through our church in Chet's name. We felt like this was an important way for the family and our church to do something possibly redemptive through this tragedy. We didn't know what to expect when we created the fund, but we had no idea how much money would actually come. Tens of thousands of dollars poured into the fund from around the country. At first, we didn't know what we were going to do with the money, but the Burchetts are so mission-minded that we knew it would go toward a meaningful mission endeavor.

It did! After nearly a year of collecting money through the fund, with the direction of the family we decided to use the money to help the Bridgeport Rescue Mission (BRM) in Bridgeport, Connecticut. Our church had a long-term relationship with BRM. Our youth had participated in cleanup projects on their campus, our laity had helped prepare meals for residents in the rehabilitation housing, our business leaders in the church led financial-planning classes for residents, and more. Many of our church members also participated in BRM's annual fundraiser for their Guest House for Women and Children. With such a deep relationship already in place, we were happy to partner with BRM in this endeavor. With over $30,000 of contributions into the memorial fund, BRM was able to completely renovate their front entryway and two main halls for adult education. The space was beautiful and communicated to all the residents in the shelter and transitional housing programs that they were important. It also provided two large meeting rooms for the residents where they could have twelve-step meetings as well as Bible studies. It was truly sacred space. When construction was complete, dozens of our members came to the consecration of the newly renovated facilities. These rooms continue to serve as gateways to wholeness for the clients of BRM.

Another part of the memorial fund that was donated to BRM was earmarked for legal expungement for those who had formerly been convicted of a crime and continued to live under the shame and shadow of what they had done. This expungement fund came as a result of Chet's experience with the justice system. His time in jail was difficult. He paid for the crime he committed with a month in jail. But once someone has completed a sentence for a crime, that crime should not follow the person for the rest of their life and prohibit them from getting gainful employment. This expungement fund helped pay attorneys working on behalf of BRM residents who were trying to get their lives in order. In both the renovation of space and the expungement fund,

Chet's memory is alive in every person who walks through those doors seeking a better life.

These two avenues through BRM were just two ways that we tried to build something meaningful out of tragedy. In the aftermath of loss, this gave all of us at church something good on which to focus our attention. It also gave us something constructive to do. This action-oriented approach, while not a magic wand for grief, can be a healthy coping mechanism. According to the National Suicide Prevention Alliance, "It can feel as if you have to do something in order to make some tiny bit of sense out of what has happened: action can be comforting."[1] The mission fund and our work at BRM felt like more than making sense of what had happened. We were trying to give hope to whoever may have felt at the end of their rope.

Just as everyone's grief is unique to them, so is their response to grief. This was how we collectively tried to memorialize Chet. Others have other ways. A family from Canada who was trying to heal after the death of their son and brother after suicide decided to remember their son and brother through their common passion. It started with just playing golf together: "So, what better way to remember him than to golf in his memory?"[2] This turned into a larger affair when their extended family—grandparents, cousins, aunts, and uncles—turned it into an annual fundraiser. The first year they raised over $20,000 and used it to raise awareness for suicide prevention and grief recovery.

These are examples of how at least two communities collectively responded to a death by suicide. Both attempted to do something not only to remember their loved one, but to help others who were facing difficult challenges. While these are attempts to do something rather than do nothing, it is important to acknowledge that sometimes it is impossible to do anything. There are important ways that families and communities heal in the aftermath of a suicide and I do not want to create any added guilt to anyone or any community who may be still paralyzed. These examples were right for these communities. I cannot prescribe what will be right for others—either individuals or communities, but I offer our story with the hope of being helpful to others.

Notes

1. National Suicide Prevention Alliance, "Help Is at Hand: Support after Someone May Have Died by Suicide," www.nhs.uk/Livewell/Suicide/Documents/Help%20is%20at%20Hand.pdf (p. 56).

2. Centre for Addiction and Mental Health, *Hope and Healing after Suicide: A Practical Guide for People Who Have Lost Someone to Suicide in Ontario* (Ontario, Canada: CAMH Publications, 2011), 58. Available online: www.camh.ca/-/media/files/guides-and-publications/hope-and-healing-en.pdf.

10

Conclusion

More than a decade has passed since Chet died. He would be thirty years old now. While he will always be a nine-teen-year-old to those of us who remember him, what is profoundly true is that we who have stayed on this side of death and knew Chet well have lived different lives since March 1, 2009. Tragedies like this are not something you "get over"; tragedies like this change you forever. Advice to those who mourn a lost one is only as good as the advice-giver's presence throughout the ordeal. More than anything else, presence is what helps survivors move through grief and pain.

As a pastor, you want to believe that sermons matter—especially given the enormous amount of time you devote to researching and writing them every week. For Baptists, preaching is the central part of the worship service. It is why our pulpits, rather than the Lord's Supper table or even the baptistery, are in the middle of the chancel. The ministry of

the word, or the preaching event/sermon, is primary in most
Baptist churches, so I hope these sermons will be helpful to
some pastors who have to preach after a tragedy like suicide.
But even in more sermon-centric worship services, there is
no substitution for love and presence. And don't be afraid to
show your own pain.

Of all the events that happened the week following Chet's
death, one conversation still stands out. I was talking with
Chet's father. He and Marcy were suffering the most through
this ordeal, so I tried not to cry in front of them. Being
natural caregivers, they would try to pastor me and take care
of me. On this occasion I was talking to "Big Chet" about the
funeral arrangements, and something in the specifics of the
funeral service cut me right to my heart. I actually remember
a sharp pain in the middle of my chest. Tears welled in my
eyes and I couldn't stop them. I told Chet I was sorry for
crying and had been trying not to cry in front of him and
Marcy. He looked at me and told me never to apologize for
crying for his son. We held each other and cried hard, big
tears.

Don't be afraid to mourn in front of your congregation.
There is a difference between "bleeding" on your parishioners and suffering with them. The first is a bid for pity; the
other shows compassion and empathy. It is important to
know the difference when you are a leader of a congregation.
Everybody in your congregation wants to know what you
think about any particular issue. Many want to know so that
they can determine if you are on their side or not. There is
a balance in this relationship between professional distance
and true pastoral care. Pastors are not therapists and should
not try to be unless they are trained as such. For most parishioners, pastors represent proximity to the divine. Pastors are
the experts on God and the representatives of God's insti-
tutions on earth. In moments of crisis, your office is deeply
meaningful to parishioners and the public. A misstep at a

funeral can turn people away from the church for the rest of their lives. It is in these critical moments when a pastor has the greatest capacity to be an agent of change for the good.

I do not wish to shy away from the reason this book exists. A young man, in his worst mental health, took his own life. These sermons were a way our congregation and I dealt with Chet's death in the immediate aftermath. Suicide prevention is the primary vehicle to make sure books like this are no longer necessary, and there are many resources. The quickest and most available is the National Suicide Prevention Lifeline: 1-800-273-8255 and/or their website: suicidepreventionlife-line.org. These lifelines are always open, they are free, and they are confidential. One of the most common things I heard—and felt—in the wake of Chet's death was "I can't believe he killed himself!" If you are struggling with suicidal ideation, please reach out for help. Use the resources that are available and look for support. I wish Chet had called me. I wish I had known he was in such a dark place. Everybody who loved him wishes the same thing. None of us wanted to live our lives without Chet, and the people in your life want you in their lives as well. If you are contemplating harming yourself, please know there are people who love you. Even when it's hard to see, your life has value.

Churches can be a real place of healing or a terrible place of trauma. Albert Y. Hsu has a wildly practical approach to how the church handles suffering. Understanding that "suffering is normative, not exceptional," Hsu gives practical advice to the church: "If there is suffering in the world, we act to relieve it. When we see disease and injury, we work to bring healing and recovery. When we encounter famine, we feed the hungry. When we see injustice and oppression, we expose it and denounce it. And when we experience grief and loss, we offer comfort."[1] It really is that simple. Offering comfort to those who are suffering the loss of a loved one is always better than trying to find out why things happen and who's at fault and how to get over it. People try to help in many ways but often provide pithy advice that comes from a good heart but isn't thoughtful or considerate. In other cases, people just stay away from the grieving families because they don't know what to do or say, so they abandon the grieving or don't talk about the massive loss when they encounter the grieving. Both cases are an act of denial. This only compounds the grief of those who suffer loss. Not only have they lost a loved one, but now they lose a community who either won't visit them or won't say a word about the tragedy. There is nothing healing when there is a refusal to speak about the tragedy. Denial festers and ruins. Again, Hsu gives practical advice: "What can friends of survivors of suicide do for them? Pray. Listen. Send cards. Provide company. Help with practical details, funeral arrangements, food, phone calls and so on. If you don't know what to do, far better simply to say 'I don't really know what to do or say' than to not do or say anything at all. That simple admission itself communicates care and concern."[2] Saying too much—or something stupid—or not saying enough are equally bad. It's not easy to get it right because the situation is so difficult. Listening and taking your cues from the survivors and those most affected is always best.

In a strange twist of fate or an act of divine providence, Chet's father, Big Chet, wrote for our church's annual Advent devotional guide only a couple of months before his son died. His devotion focused on Luke 1:26-38, and he titled it "Love Lights Our Way." It was the devotion for the fourth Sunday in Advent 2008—the Sunday of Love. It is fitting to end this book with Big Chet's faith. These were his words when his son was in jail, and they remained a deep part of his faith even after Chet died.

But wait, cruelty, anger and vengeance are often the norm today—in countries far away and in homes just down the street. Mothers kneel over graves in desolate grief, their children lost to war or disease or drugs. In our world today, millions are starving. And in our immediate community the homeless will shiver tonight and the hungry will ache. Jesus' advent changed potential for us and our world, but the brokenness remains. . . . We should consider that the light of God's love can only shine today if we carry it forward in our faith, conduct and service. Our willingness to be vessels for Christ's love is as important today as was Mary's willingness to be the vessel for God's son. Our world is different because in His love, God chose to make Himself part of our existence. But we must lift the light of that love above today's darkness. It's up to us to demonstrate the reality of God's love in the world and allow Him to keep changing lives. Maybe it seems daunting to consider our individual role in God's plan. It must have been quite a shock for Mary. But then again, as the angel said, "Nothing is impossible with God" (Luke 1:37). Oh God, may we be reminded today that nothing is impossible with you! Amen.[3]

Notes

1. Albert Y. Hsu, *Grieving a Suicide: A Loved One's Search for Comfort, Answers, and Hope* (Downers Grove, IL: IVP Books, 2002), 129.

2. Ibid., 143.

3. Chet Burchett, "Love Lights Our Way," in *2008 Advent Devotional Guide: Wilton Baptist Church* (Wilton, CT: privately printed by Wilton Baptist Church, 2008), 32–33.

Resources

Suicide Prevention

Books

Blauner, Susan Rose. *How I Stayed Alive When My Brain Was Trying to Kill Me: One Person's Guide to Suicide Prevention.* San Francisco: Harper Collins, 2009.

Button, Mark E., and Ian Marsh, eds. *Suicide and Social Justice: New Perspectives on the Politics of Suicide and Suicide Prevention.* Oxford: Routledge, 2019.

Falcone, Tatiana, and Jane Timmons-Mitchell, eds. *Suicide Prevention: A Practical Guide for the Practitioner.* Cham, Switzerland: Springer, 2018.

Knapp, Samuel J. *Suicide Prevention: An Ethically and Scientifically Informed Approach.* Washington, DC: American Psychological Association, 2019.

Mason, Karen. *Preventing Suicide: A Handbook for Pastors, Chaplains and Pastoral Counselors.* Downers Grove, IL: Inter Varsity Press, 2014.

Page, Andrew C., and Werner G. K. Stritzke, eds. *Alternatives to Suicide: Beyond Risk and toward a Life Worth Living.* London: Academic Press, 2020.

Organizations

Crisis Text Line
Text HOME to 741741 or visit www.crisistextline.org/

National Institute of Mental Health (NIMH)
www.nimh.nih.gov/health/topics/suicide-prevention/
index.shtml

National Suicide Prevention Lifeline
suicidepreventionlifeline.org/
800-273-8255
Online chat: suicidepreventiononline.org/

Society for the Prevention of Teen Suicide
www.sptsusa.org/

Substance Abuse and Mental Health Services
Administration (SAMHSA)
Offers services in both English and Spanish
www.samhsa.gov/find-help/national-helpline
800-662-4357

Suicide Prevention Resource Center
www.sprc.org

Trevor Project
Specifically offers help to LGBTQ+ youth.
www.thetrevorproject.org/
Text START to 678678 or call 866-488-7386

Grief and Pastoral Care

Books

Bowler, Kate. *Everything Happens for a Reason: And Other Lies I've Loved*. New York: Random House, 2018.

Haugk, Kenneth C. *Christian Caregiving: A Way of Life*. Minneapolis: Augsburg, 1984.

———. *Journeying through Grief*. St. Louis, MO: Stephens Ministries, 2004.

Hickman, Martha Whitmore. *Healing after Loss: Daily Meditations for Working through Grief*. New York: William Morrow, 1994.

Hunt, Gregory L. *Leading Congregations through Crisis*. St. Louis, MO: Chalice Press, 2012.

Kalanithi, Paul. *When Breath Becomes Air: What Makes Life Worth Living in the Face of Death*. New York: Vintage, 2016.

Nordal, Katherine C. "Grief: Coping with the Loss of Your Loved One." In American Psychological Association. www.apa.org/topics/grief. January 1, 2020.

Rowland, Joanna. *The Memory Box: A Book about Grief*. Minneapolis: Sparkhouse Family, 2017.

Rupp, Joyce. *Praying Our Goodbyes: A Spiritual Companion through Life's Losses and Sorrows.* Notre Dame, IN: Ava Maria Press, 2012.

Schultz, Richard. *The Psychology of Death, Dying, and Bereavement.* Reading, MA: Addison-Wesley, 1978.

Organizations

The Center for Complicated Grief
complicatedgrief.columbia.edu/professionals/
complicated-grief-professionals/overview/

Stephen Ministries
www.stephenministries.org

Theodicy

Jorgensen, Larry M., and Samuel Newlands, eds. *New Essays on Leibniz's Theodicy.* Oxford: Oxford University Press, 2014.

Kropf, Richard W. *Evil and Evolution: A Theodicy.* Eugene, OR: Wipf and Stock, 2004.

Leibniz, Gottfried Wilhelm. *Theodicy: Essays on the Goodness of God, the Freedom of Man, and the Origin of Evil.* E. M. Huggard, trans. Austin M. Farrer, ed. New York: Cosimo Classics, 2009 (originally published 1710).

Yancey, Philip. *Disappointment with God: Three Questions No One Asks Aloud.* Grand Rapids, MI: Zondervan, 1988.

———. *Where Is God When It Hurts?* Grand Rapids, MI: Zondervan, 1990.

Bibliography

Burchett, Chet. "Love Lights Our Way." In 2008 Advent Devotional Guide: Wilton Baptist Church. Wilton, CT: Privately Printed by Wilton Baptist Church, 2008. Used with permission from the author.

Castelo, Daniel. *Theological Theodicy.* Cascade Companions 14; Eugene, OR: Cascade Books, 2012.

Center for Complicated Grief, "Key Definitions," complicatedgrief.columbia.edu/professionals/complicated-grief-professionals/overview/, accessed on April 22, 2020.

Centre for Addiction and Mental Health. Hope and Healing after Suicide: A Practical Guide for People Who Have Lost Someone to Suicide in Ontario. Ontario, Canada: CAMH Publications, 2011.

Crenshaw, James L. *Defending God: Biblical Responses to the Problem of Evil.* Oxford and New York: Oxford University Press, 2005.

Farley, Margaret A. "Theological Perspective: John 12:20-33." In *Feasting on the Word: Preaching the Revised Common Lectionary*, edited by David L. Bartlett and Barbara Brown Taylor. Year B, Volume 2; Louisville: Westminster John Knox Press, 2008.

Harari, Yuval Noah. *Sapiens: A Brief History of Humankind*. New York: Harper Collins Publishing, 2015.

Hayes, Steven C., Kirk D. Strosahl, and Kelly G. Wilson, eds. *Acceptance and Commitment Therapy: The Process and Practice of Mindful Change*. 2nd ed. New York: The Guilford Press, 2012.

Hsu, Albert Y. *Grieving a Suicide: A Loved One's Search for Comfort, Answers & Hope*. Downers Grove, IL: IVP Books, 2002.

Iceland, John. *Poverty in America: A Handbook*. Berkley: University of California Press, 2006.

Jaffe, Eric. "Why Love Literally Hurts." In Association for Psychological Science (February, 2013), www.psychologicalscience.org/observer/why-love-literally-hurts, accessed on April 16, 2020.

Kaiser Family Foundation, "COVID-19 Coronavirus Tracker—Updated as of April 22, 2020." www.kff.org/global-health-policy/fact-sheet/coronavirus-tracker/, accessed on April 22, 2020.

Kerouac, Jack. *On the Road*. London: Penguin Books, 1959.

Kübler-Ross, Elisabeth. *On Death and Dying: What the Dying Have to Teach Doctors, Nurses, Clergy and Their Own Families*. New York: Macmillan, 1970.

Lesser, Elizabeth. *Broken Open: How Difficult Times Can Help Us Grow*. New York: Villard, 2005.

Lewis, C. S. *A Grief Observed.* 1961; repr., San Francisco: Harper San Francisco, 2001.

————. *The Problem of Pain.* 1940; repr., San Francisco: Harper San Francisco, 2001.

Luoma, Jason B., Steven C. Hayes, and Robyn D. Walser, eds. *Learning ACT: An Acceptance & Commitment Therapy Skills Training Manual for Therapists.* 2nd ed. Oakland, CA: Context Press, 2017.

Miłosz, Czesław. Nobel Lecture. Delivered on December 8, 1980, www.nobelprize.org/prizes/literature/1980/milosz/lecture/.

National Suicide Prevention Alliance. "Help Is at Hand: Support after Someone May Have Died by Suicide." www.nhs.uk/Livewell/Suicide/Documents/Help%20is%20at%20Hand.pdf.

Nouwen, Henri J. M. *The Wounded Healer: Ministry in Contemporary Society.* New York: Doubleday, 1972.

Olivea, Gordon. "Brazilian Sunset," written June 4, 1998. Used with permission from the author.

————. "One Strong Leg," written June 2, 1998. Used with permission from the author.

Payne Ruby K., and Bill Ehlig. *What Every Church Member Should Know about Poverty.* Highlands, TX: RFT Publishing Co., 1999.

Poole, Charles E. *A Church for Rachel: Sermons for Those Who Mourn.* Macon, GA: Mercer University Press, 2012.

Scott, Mark S. *Pathways in Theodicy: An Introduction to the Problem of Pain.* Minneapolis: Fortress Press, 2015.

Taylor, Barbara Brown "Our Bodies, Our Faith: Practicing Incarnation" in *Christian Century* (January 27, 2009), www.christiancentury.org/article/2009-01/our-bodies-our-faith.

Ward, Jesmyn. *Men We Reaped: A Memoir.* New York: Bloomsbury, 2013.

Westberg, Grander E. *Good Grief.* Minneapolis: Fortress Press, 1997.